Guiding Their Way
DAY BY DAY

Glo Wellman

Outskirts Press, Inc.
Denver, Colorado

Outskirts Press, Inc.
http://www.outskirtspress.com

ISBN: 978-1-4327-3647-7

Library of Congress Control Number: 2008940476

Outskirts Press and the "OP" logo are trademarks belonging to Outskirts Press, Inc.

PRINTED IN THE UNITED STATES OF AMERICA

Introduction

A book goes through a birthing process. Dreams and reality come together. With times of joy and times of frustration, plus a healthy dose of wonder and imagination, the writing meets the page. Pages come together, then pictures, and with some pushing and screaming, a finished creation is born.

Along the way, just like in life, some doubts can surface. "Who am I to publish a book with ideas about raising children?" I have definitely made mistakes as a mom. I still do. My life is far from perfect. My adult children have been through rocky times. And then my oldest son said to me, "Who better to write this?"

I often hold myself to unreasonable expectations. Perfection is impossible. In truth, I have done the best I could in the moment, and my heart has been my guide, even when I was misguided. Remembering to be gentle with myself has been one of my on-going challenges. We all have doubts about our ability to be effective guardians for children. Questioning helps us to stay open to learning and mastering our skills.

No child comes to us with an instruction book. If they did, it could not be mass produced, but rather would need to be personalized because each child has unique needs and abilities. Even with knowledge as a teacher and experience as the "Big Sister" in my family, nothing could really prepare me for the joys and pain, the wonders and the challenges of raising a child. Each of my sons was a mystery. Each child is a mystery. So we must prepare to be surprised!

We come from varied childhood experiences. Some of us are fortunate to have had wonderful childhoods and positive role models. Others did not. Some of us have a strong network that offers assistance and emotional support. Others feel more isolated and alone. We all need a wise village around us to share the responsibilities of child rearing – family, friends, schools, and community.

We want the best for children. We have their healthy development at the heart of our interactions. We may feel like we know what they need, but we don't always remember in the moment. Stresses and pressures work on us and we forget our best intentions. We snap or yell or hurry children along. This book is meant to be an encouraging reminder that children are awesome beings. Each child is born with a unique potential based on temperament, curiosity, creativity, energy, and abilities.

Life is a journey and sometimes a perilous one. There are many twists and turns along the way. And certainly, the responsibility of being a parent, a grandparent, or a teacher is full of challenges. We can't determine any child's future. But we can love them. We can try to understand them. We can make choices that we hope will help them eventually develop into the people they were meant to be. All we can really do is the best we can do, one step at a time. One moment at a time. One day at a time.

How you read this book is up to you. Daily. Many pages at a time. Or just open the book to any page. These brief readings are offered to strengthen your resolve, boost your energy, and refocus your thoughts. Some of these readings will be just what you wanted to hear. Some will frustrate you. Some will bring tears. Some will bring you joy and remind you of the precious lives you hold in trust. My hope is that something in these pages will bring you increased confidence in the love you feel for children. So that with an open heart, you can take the next step in this journey, and be there for a child.

January

Our Journey Begins

The day our child comes into our life, we rarely imagine the wild ride ahead. There will be highs and lows we never expected. There will be surprising curves that take us places we have not anticipated.

Being entrusted with the care of a child is an awesome responsibility and a tender gift. There are challenging times that will drain all of our energy and rewarding moments when we feel our heart may burst. In the long run, the rewards far outweigh the struggles and disappointments.

We will travel together during this coming year. We haven't been given a road map, so we will need to stay open and flexible for what is ahead.

With love as our guide and children as our teachers, we can figure out what is best for us all.

New Year Resolutions

Many of us have made countless promises for the new year. And several weeks or months down the road, we find ourselves slipping. Our resolutions were probably unrealistic. We were hoping against hope that this time we might be able to keep them, that this time we might be able to reach perfection.

That really is silly, isn't it? None of us will ever be perfect. But our resolutions can be goals that we hold before us. We can continue to strive for the health and happiness we long to experience.

You can decide whether you will create some of your own goals for this year. But, since this book is for adults who care for children, here are a few "resolutions" which will be revisited within these pages.

1) What's the hurry? Slow down and play more.
2) See the world through a child's eyes and learn.
3) Give children the focused attention they need.
4) Remember – They learn from what we say and do.

5) Self-care is not selfish!

6) Practice an attitude of gratitude.

Children need adults in their lives who are modeling the qualities which are needed to create a healthy, fulfilling life.

Children Can't Wait   JANUARY 3

They do – all the time! They wait for us.

"Wait a minute. I need to finish this first."

"I'll be there in a bit."

Children need to learn to wait. After the dependency of infancy, toddlers learn that the world does not revolve around them. Children need to learn to wait their turn. They want that toy now. Waiting is hard. Ask any adult who is stuck in a long line or in traffic.

Sometimes children can't wait. The bathroom isn't close enough when they need it. Where is food when they are hungry?

There are also critical periods for learning. Sometimes children are eager to have their questions answered, "Why?" At other times, all of their patience and curiosity are focused on paying attention to their current fun activity.

Sometimes they really can't wait!

They can't wait to know we love them!

They can't wait to tell us a story.

They can't wait to give us a hug!

Children need to learn to wait. But, their childhoods pass quickly. Each child needs to realize he is special.

Children can't wait!

Discipline with Love   JANUARY 4

Many of us are confused about the concept of discipline. Some of us experienced harsh punishment when growing up, and still feel the sting. We don't want children to know this kind of adult reaction. Some of us had no limits and no parental voice to guide, so we felt the consequences of our own choices. How are we to discipline children today?

The word "discipline" actually comes from the same root as "disciple." A disciple is someone who follows a beloved teacher. Children admire and look up to us. We have a responsibility to offer them the guidance and respect they deserve.

Our best discipline comes from the heart and is rooted in love –

We want children to be safe.

We want them to grow into healthy adults.

We want them to have the resources to be all
they can be.

We can't know for sure what children will become when they reach adulthood. We *can* offer a variety of opportunities which encourage their learning and growth. We *can* do our best now to provide love and limits.

The Basics JANUARY 5

Children need adult support to help them learn how to behave appropriately. Adults need some tools to guide children in positive and healthy ways. These tools are simple, but their application requires consistency and sensitivity.

Basic Tools for guiding children will be reinforced throughout this book.

> *Know the Child* – Every child is unique. Every situation is different. We can observe children to figure out the reasons behind the behaviors and then decide what is needed.

> *Communication and Listening* – The most important part of communication is listening. We can take the time to hear what children are saying. What do they need? What is important to them? What is frustrating to them?

> *Encouragement* – We all appreciate positive feedback. Acknowledging strengths helps us learn.

Redirection – It is not enough to *just say "No."* Children have a one track mind. When they are into something that is not appropriate, we need to direct them to another acceptable activity.

First Things First – Some things need to be done before play. "You can do that as soon as you finish."

Self-Care – If we forget to take care of ourselves, we will not have the energy or patience to take care of children.

We are teachable, too. What we say and do influences children.

Attention – Understanding Needs JANUARY 6

Children want attention. "Attention" means "I need something. Please help me out."

Sometimes children use words to tell us what they need. But, often their behaviors cry out – "Help!" Their actions might be saying –

I need to be held.
I'm tired. Please be patient with me.
I need acceptable choices.
I'm hungry.
I need to be reminded of the rules.
I'm feeling frustrated.
I need time to work through this.

If we react without thinking about what the behavior might be telling us, our response is not likely to be effective. But, when we consider children's needs, the chance of a successful solution is more likely.

Children's needs can often be answered pretty simply with our focused attention, eye contact, a caring voice, and a prompt response. If we try to put them off too long, their behavior can escalate and we *both* become more frustrated.

First Things First

Children go from one activity to the next without much thought about clean up or other plans. They want to do what they want to do when they want to do it.

There is an order to life that we adults usually figure out. We have schedules and know that certain activities naturally come first. This ability to find the order in things is rarely an innate skill. It is learned. Children need our help to understand.

"First things first" is a request that can be used to guide a child's choices and activities. When a child wants to do something and the timing isn't right, we can say, "First we need to finish this activity and clean up, and then you can do that." This implies:

Homework before TV
Breakfast before play
Chores before going outside to play
Bath and story before bedtime
Clean up before the next activity

Our routines and sense of timing can help create harmony in our busy life. First things first.

Small Steps

A baby learns to walk in small steps. First crawling, then pulling up to a standing position, holding on while cruising the furniture. Toddlers spend a lot of time practicing, standing, finally letting go and balancing. The child's expression of joy and excitement says, "Look at me – I did it!"

Then come the first small, cautious steps, sometimes almost by accident. Before our eyes, our little one is off and running. Confidence builds. Steps become more steady. "Look at me – I did it!"

This same process will be repeated throughout a lifetime as new things are learned: the first words, then sentences; stacking blocks; walking home from school alone; learning to read; excelling at a sport; learning to drive.

The instant the new learning is realized is an "Aha!" moment. That moment has actually been supported by many previous tiny steps and much trial and error...trying and trying again.

My Way! JANUARY 9

Adults can be incredibly stubborn at times. After years of doing it *my way*, we resist a new approach. Hmm. Maybe there is a clue here to where children get their persistence.

Children want us to be open to their ideas. They can be very determined teachers. They are trying to train us all the time. They are trying to teach us how to help them when they're angry. They are telling us what they will not eat. They let us know what they need.

When we stubbornly insist on doing it *my way*, power struggles erupt as we butt heads with an equally determined child. Our actions are saying, "I don't care what you need right now, this is how we are going to do this!" And guess what? Predictably, we get an argument.

In any situation, we can only really change ourselves and our reaction. And if we do, miracles can happen. When we do it differently, others often change in response to our unexpected behavior. We can insist that it be *my way* or we can be open and willing to try something new.

Another Way JANUARY 10

When we are in the midst of a conflict, the best solution is to find *another way*. We do this by being flexible and offering limited choices.

You want an eight o'clock bedtime. Your child is resisting. You can fight and get her into bed with screaming on both sides, or you can negotiate a slight adjustment that is workable for both of you. "It's eight o'clock. I want to read your bedtime story now. You want to stay up. How about we set the timer for ten more minutes. Then, we'll read one story."

Often, children will agree to this slight adjustment. When the ten minutes have passed, they go off to bed without a fight.

Sometimes we cannot find another way. We are late and have no time. Or it is a safety issue and "No, absolutely not!" is the appropriate response.

But, when we can, a little flexibility goes a long way toward making a more peaceful resolution.

I Was So Embarrassed JANUARY 11

> Your child throws a fit in the store because you won't buy the cookies that are on display at the end of the aisle.
>
> You have company visiting and your grandson will not share any of his toys.
>
> Your teen yells at you in front of the neighbors, "Get out of my life!"

There are many potentially embarrassing moments with children. Though these can be frustrating, we can respond calmly. We can learn to *not* take these experiences personally. Children's reactions are rarely intentionally meant to embarrass us. They are feeling overwhelmed, frustrated, or hungry and don't think about the social significance of this behavior.

When these moments occur, take a breath. Imagine how your child is feeling. Acknowledge this. "I can tell you are very disappointed." Then, redirect your child to a different focus or activity.

We can choose to be embarrassed. Or we can choose to be understanding.

"I'm the Big Sister!" JANUARY 12

There she is, pushing the stroller with her little sister sleeping inside. As neighbors pass by, she proudly says, "I'm the big sister!" Right now, this is fun. She is proud of herself.

She may also feel protective and responsible.

Later, that same Big Sister can be very angry when little sister interferes with her play. Or Big Sister can break down at the end of a day and sob sadly when she has to go to bed before little sister who is being rocked and nursed to sleep.

Big Sister is only three years old. It's hard to be Big Sister or Big Brother all of the time. Sometimes Big Sister needs to be taken care of, too. She wants to be held and rocked.

Our realistic expectations can help. Children eventually grow up. But, being responsible all of the time can be a big burden. Older siblings need time to be kids – to play and fuss and laugh and cry. We can shape our expectations to match each child's needs.

Cherish the Moments   JANUARY 13

Time flies...way too quickly!! Before we realize it, children have reached another milestone. Then it seems like we just turn around and they have changed again. That accomplishment which seemed so far off is here.

When we are in the middle of hard times, it feels like these difficulties will not end. But, they do. If we're not careful, our busy lives consume us and *we* are the ones who have missed their childhood.

What can we do to cherish the moments we have? "I'm too busy. I can't right now." Is that really true? A few minutes spent together now can be like money invested well. Children want to spend time with us and are often content to be with us as we do chores or go shopping. We can make these ordinary activities fun. When children are older and start to push us away, they will still be more likely to turn to us when they need some help if we have consistently made ourselves available.

Work on a joint project, make cookies together, or take a short walk. We don't need to go out of our way to do special things, but we can do our best to make many of the ordinary moments in a day memorable!

Good Morning

"Come on! Get up! We're going to be late again." We rush around, yelling, fussing, stalling. Finally out the door and into the car, everyone is hassled. What a way to start the morning! *Let's try again.*

As usual, we have another full day ahead. Children don't have a clue about everything we have to do to get going on time. But, we will almost always get a more cheerful, cooperative response from children if we greet the day together with love and a smile.

Rubbing his back, "Good morning. How's my sweet boy this morning?" He yawns and stretches, rewarding you with a sleepy smile. "Let's get dressed so we can eat some breakfast together this morning." Giving him a squeeze, "What should we have, cereal or scrambled eggs?"

Now that's better. With gentle coaxing and support along the way, we make it out of the house on time. And all it took was love, a smile, and a little bit of creative planning. Good morning!

Our Ambivalent Feelings

Nothing can prepare us for the intense feelings that parenthood brings. Once this little person joins us, we are forever changed. Our love is stronger than we ever thought possible. We hurt more than we ever imagined.

In any given moment, our feelings can shift from one extreme to another. We quickly discover that it really is possible to love a child and at the same time be incredibly annoyed by the current misbehavior.

As we watch children grow, we experience their joys and we delight at their new accomplishments. We also feel their frustrations and disappointments. When they struggle, our heart hurts, too.

We are also capable of our own very intense feelings when children's behaviors do not match our expectations. Our ambivalent feelings are to be expected. We deserve the same acceptance, patience, and love that we offer children during challenging times.

Not Another Errand!

Most of us have felt embarrassed or frustrated with a child's behavior when we were in a public place. The store seems to entice children. They whine and fuss, demanding this treat or that toy. Waiting in line at the bank or sitting at the doctor's office, children are bored and energetic. It's hard to wait. It's impossible to sit still.

We can plan these trips to minimize hassle and maximize fun. Before going out, let children know where you are going and about how long it will take. Even small children do better when they know what to expect.

Try to arrange errands at a time of day that is good for both of you: early in the day when you are rested or at a time when you don't feel pushed by other demands.

Sometimes a stop at a park can help children burn off some extra energy. Then, the time at the store or the office goes more smoothly.

Children don't misbehave just to embarrass us. They need help to find something to do. They can learn how to behave in public settings.

Balancing Act

Have you seen a performer spinning plates on rods? He scurries between them, spinning them to keep all balancing. Or have you seen someone juggle four or five objects, keeping them all in the air? These are amazing feats that take incredible energy and focus. When they succeed, we are in awe.

Do you ever feel like you are trying to spin full plates and are barely able to keep them going? Or as if you are in the middle of a circus juggling act? Life can be both exhausting and exhilarating. Everyone has different needs and abilities. There are schedules to juggle, meals to prepare, clothes to wash, toys and clutter to clean up, all on top of our jobs.

This is where setting priorities can help us focus on the essentials. We can simplify our routines. We can maintain realistic expectations about what we can reasonably accomplish right now. We can ask for help and be willing to accept assistance. Busy lives and many needs require a careful balancing act.

Pick Your Battles   JANUARY 18

Too often we overreact to every misstep children take. We have days when we have no patience. Every time we turn around our child is doing something annoying or disobedient, testing our limits at every turn.

And as soon as we raise our battle flag and respond in anger, they prepare to defend themselves and scream back at us. "You're not my boss!!"

Battle lines are drawn and we are off to war! If we don't carefully choose our response, we could find ourselves snapping at children all day long.

Instead, we can ask ourselves, "What is really most important right now?" Certainly, not spilt milk. Certainly, not shoes left in the entry way. Certainly, not dirty dishes left in the bedroom. A simple request should solve this, "Please take a few minutes to bring your dirty clothes to the hamper so they will get washed."

What is worth fighting for? Important values of love and respect. Concerns for someone's safety. Even these things are won more effectively with patience and understanding than with a fight.

Let's Try Again   JANUARY 19

A father enjoyed taking his sons skating. But he didn't enjoy the drive. The boys, 5 and 7, would fight with each other all the way there. It was difficult for him to focus on his driving. The fighting did not start the outing off on good footing. This can be frustrating for everyone.

On one such Saturday, dad pulled over when they were screaming at each other and said, "If you guys can't be kind to each other on the way to skating, I'm going to turn around and go home." Their quiet didn't last long. A little further down the road, they were complaining at each other again. So at the next corner, dad turned the car around. "No! We'll be nice dad! Please!" He calmly said, "Sorry guys, I like skating too, but maybe next time we'll be able to get there peacefully." And home they went. Dad *and* the boys were disappointed.

They did go again the next weekend. And this time dad said, "Remember how last week I went back home because you guys were fighting? Well, we're going to try again. And this time I hope you two can be kind to each other on the way there." Not surprisingly, they were. And they all had a good time.

We want to have fun with children, but it doesn't always go as we hope. Sometimes they need a consequence to finally get it. The next time, they often make better choices.

Reading Together JANUARY 20

A love of reading will open a child's life to a world of possibilities. Most school subjects are tied to reading. Experts recognize that one of the most important things we can do to insure a child's future success is to read to them.

We can make reading together a habit that need not cost anything. Public libraries are great resources. Children's librarians know books and can help us find the right one.

The words and images in a book come alive as children imagine the setting and characters. What are they doing? What does this fictional world look like? Children who enjoy reading often have a vivid imagination. Their creativity allows them to fantasize other possibilities.

What are your child's favorite books? What books did you enjoy as a child? Reading is a way to connect and spend some quality time together. Find a comfortable spot, snuggle up, and lose yourselves in the pages of a book.

Learning from the Past JANUARY 21

How we were raised influences today's choices. The environment we grew up in, the friends we had, and our family life, all shaped our expectations.

You may have been a child who needed to take care of yourself. If your homework got done at all, it was entirely up to you. Or you may have had parents who were overly attentive and made your choices for you. So now that you have children of your own, you aren't sure what would be best for them.

No matter what life was like, we can figure out what is best for us today. There are many different ways to be a family. We need to be willing to look at our own past and consider whether those experiences can help us as we guide children, or whether we need to try new things.

Part of raising children is about growing up ourselves, looking at our own experiences with a more realistic eye, and choosing to discover what will work for us today.

Rescuing "Should" JANUARY 22

We have experienced many "shoulds" in our lifetime and they still guide our decisions.

> I really should lose a few pounds.
> I shouldn't buy that because...
> You should remember to...

The internal message that we sometimes come to believe is that, "You need to give up that thing which you really love or do something that you really don't want to do because others are expecting it."

"Should" often feels like a judgment. We feel pressured into doing something that really doesn't seem right for us. Sometimes we "should" ourselves into shouldering *all* the responsibility for our family's well-being.

"Should" is the past tense of "shall" which means *intend to* or *plan to*. We can rescue "should" from someone else's expectations for us, and convert this into a statement that reflects what we know is right.

I should and I shall read to my child today.
I should and I shall walk daily.
I should and I shall join a singing group.

Our own positive "shoulds" can help us to live a more intentional life, planning for those activities which are right for us!

Good Girl

There is no such thing as a bad kid. All children are good kids even though they sometimes behave badly. It is important to separate the child from the behavior.

We give children positive feedback when we are pleased with what they have done. This encourages them to repeat appropriate behavior. But, comments that focus on character are tricky. We mean well when we say, "You're such a good girl." But, all too soon, children have a voice *inside* which reflects something very different – "No, I'm not really so good. She is forgetting when I got in trouble. I was bad then."

Even positive labels like "good girl" are a judgment. It is uncomfortable to feel judged or evaluated. Children need our help to develop positive internal messages. When we express our appreciation, children learn what behavior is appropriate and why. A child's internal thoughts are most helpful in shaping positive learning and self-esteem.

"Thank you for putting your dishes in the sink."
Internal – "I am capable."
"I'm happy to hear you two laughing together."
Internal – "Todd and I can have fun together."

Children learn from encouraging words that show we care.

Learning to Be a "Daddy"

There is a popular phrase:

> "Anyone can be a father, but it takes
> someone special to be a Daddy."

Little boys are encouraged from an early age to be independent and think for themselves. They are taught to be responsible. Sometimes when our sons are young, we wonder if they will ever get it. We wonder what they will be like as a father.

Boys learn about being a parent through role modeling. What are their fathers like? What about their grandfathers, or the fathers of their friends, or their teachers who are men? What are they learning from the men in their lives about being a responsible *and* nurturing adult?

Boys *and* girls both need positive male role models in their lives. They need men who are willing to show their love. They need men who can talk about their feelings. They need men who know how to take care of themselves. They need men who know how to resolve conflicts in healthy ways.

Children need men in their lives who can offer their love and support in many ways.

Temperature's Rising!

Your child is restless, whiny, and demanding! You're tired, too, so this brings out the worst in you. You have no patience and bedtime becomes a disaster. Finally, your child falls asleep. Then, in the middle of the night, you are awakened by tears. As you hold your child, the fever is obvious. Now, the evening's behavior is explained.

This happens to all of us, children and adults. We start to feel crabby and disagreeable *before* the signs of illness show up. One of the life lessons then is to try to respond to children with patience – at all times. Since we're not always perfect, there is a way to put the previous night behind us. Show patience now.

Once a cold or other illness has crept in, TLC is the prescription for the day. We all need Tender, Loving Care! Rest, calm activities, light, simple meals, and lots of patience. An illness usually takes its course in a few days. We can't hurry this, but we can delay it if we push ourselves.

We also need to remember to strengthen ourselves against getting sick. Wash your hands frequently and rest when the sick child is resting.

Letting Go with Love JANUARY 26

At many points during children's development, we need to remember to let go as they learn to do things on their own and take responsibility for their own choices. We let go...

When she takes her first steps.
As he walks to school, alone.
When she is angry at a friend and there is
    nothing we can do to fix it.
When he can't find something in his messy
    room.
When she is not selected for the team.
When homework isn't turned in on time.

Letting go is hard. We have such strong hopes for children. We want them to feel comfortable and confident. We want them to do well and succeed. And, we are often under the false impression that we have some kind of power to control their future or determine a safe outcome. We don't. We *can* establish a firm foundation based in love, positive values, life skills, choices, and decision making. Then we step back with the knowledge that children have the skills needed to proceed with independence.

Letting go does not mean we abandon them when our support would be helpful. We remain available. Letting go with love says, "Even though this is hard or frustrating for you, I know you can do this. You can figure this out. I believe in you."

Valuing Our Role as "Parent"

Life is full. We work hard. From dawn until our head hits the pillow and sleep takes over, we are moving. We feel many pressures on our time and energies. In addition to family life, we have job demands and school issues, medical appointments and home chores.

We don't always feel appreciated as parents. Sometimes we feel pressured by others to do more with little recognition of the impact this can have on the family life. It is no surprise that we sometimes wonder how we will manage it all.

In reality, there is no job or responsibility that is more important than that of *Parent*. Children need us to care for them and tend to the many details of life. They need us to love them unconditionally. They need us to set limits. We teach them about relationships, about commitment, about cooperation, about responsibility.

We will not have the energy to sustain all of this if we are tired, sick, and impatient. We must value and take care of ourselves. Laughing together and having fun also helps us as we move through our day.

Nurturing adults are very important in the life of a child.

Trusting

Trust develops over time. Children learn to trust us and we learn to trust them. Our consistent behavior helps them learn to depend upon us. Our daily experiences with them tell us what we can reasonably expect from them.

The most important first step for trusting is being trustworthy ourselves. If we don't follow through with what we say and do, children will not learn to be consistent either.

Trusting is also felt through our communication. When we talk honestly and openly with children, we get to know each other. We discover who they are and what they believe in.

We want to believe him when he says his homework is done. We want to trust that her chores have been completed. It is normal for children to test limits a little. So, we do need to check it out. "Okay, let's have a look." If the task is completed, "Good job. Thanks for helping the family out." If it is not, "Ah, I know you wish it was done, but it's not. Do you need some help or can you do it yourself right now?"

Trusting is an important part of our relationships with children. Trust grows over time.

Trouble with Transitions   JANUARY 29

Young children have a hard time moving from one activity to the next. When they are involved with an activity, they are often deep into it, body and soul! We come along with our own plans. Without consulting them or giving any kind of warning, we ask them – no – we demand that they stop what they are doing right now!

How many adults respond well to this kind of interruption? *Stop! Stop now! And do what I want.* Not many of us would receive this request cheerfully. It's hard for children, too.

Giving a little warning helps to ease the transition. Warnings prepare the child for what lies ahead.

> "In ten minutes, we're going to clean up and get
> ready for _____ ."

Routines also help children know what to expect. When we have a consistent schedule, they are not as surprised by the need to stop what they are doing to move to the next thing.

When we experience resistance, we can acknowledge the child's feelings, "I know this isn't what you expected. What can I do to help you get ready?" As we become more understanding, and they mature, children also learn to be more flexible and cooperative.

Recovery Parenting   JANUARY 30

All parents have a full time job – 24 hours, 7 days a week. Recovery from addictions also requires a total commitment.

So, *Recovery Parenting* is 24 x 7 x 2. Impossible? No, but very demanding!

Some parents are in recovery from hurtful childhoods or addictive behaviors. Parents new to recovery have the added pressures that their children often bring to the mix. Mom or dad is very different now, clean and sober. She looks different, and talks differently. Dad notices things that he let slide in the past, or perhaps was totally unaware of.

Parents in recovery are setting many new boundaries and limits for themselves and their children. Reminders in the recovery program can help *all* of us maintain a healthy life for ourselves and our children.

> *One day at a time* – Each day is a new day. Stay in the present and focus on what is needed right now.
>
> *Support is a must* – We are not meant to go through this alone. Cultivate relationships with friends and family who are willing to help.
>
> *Progress not perfection* – One step at a time. Positive growth starts with baby steps forward.
>
> *Self-care is not selfish* – Recovery demands that we take care of ourselves with sleep, healthy food, and exercise.

The steps which support recovery also help us be the best we can be.

The Important Stuff   JANUARY 31

There are little things that irritate us. But in the long run, do they really matter? In five years, will it really matter that...

> Your child spilled milk at most meals for
>   months.
> You couldn't get him to bathe very regularly.
> Your grandson wants to shave his head.
> Your daughter wants a nose stud.

What is really important? What is going to make a difference when you look back on these times? What *does* matter is that...

> We spend time together doing child-chosen activities.
>
> Children feel comfortable coming to us about anything, knowing we will listen.
>
> We change our schedule to attend school events.
>
> We demonstrate unconditional love often – no matter what.

This is the *important stuff*. This is how we show children that we know what really matters.

February

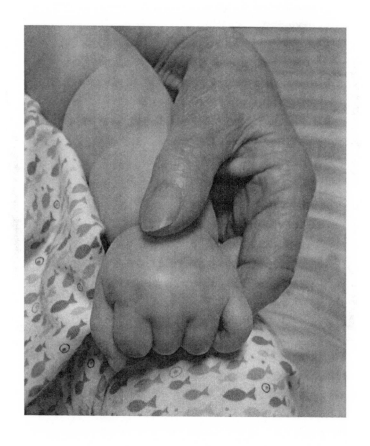

Job Description – Parent

Immediate opening for someone who will attend to the needs of a child. This child tests every boundary and explores all "off limits" places. This child can be busy, demanding, inquisitive, creative, independent, fun-loving, and intense.

Requirements of the job –

> Full-time live-in work; On call: 24-7;
>
> No experience required – on the job training;
>
> Be willing to drop what you are doing at any moment;
>
> Sharp-witted and responsive; Must think on your feet; Quick reflexes;
>
> General maintenance: cook, shop, clean-up, chauffeur;
>
> Health care expert; School tutor; Law enforcer; Negotiator; Diplomat;
>
> Good sense of humor;
>
> Magician and miracle worker.

Benefits and rewards –

> Priceless smiles and hugs;
>
> Unconditional love;
>
> Opportunities for creativity;
>
> Watching a child grow and blossom.

Children Change Us

That's an understatement! Before we became parents, we may have naively believed we would continue as we had. Yes, a little person is coming to join us, but what difference can eight pounds make? What a surprise is ahead for us!

We go from our B.C. (Before Children) selves, focusing on our work and our own interests to full-time parenthood. Now, we still have lots of work to do, but very little time for personal needs. The daily chores of life still call to us – meals, clothing, cleaning, appointments. We also focus large amounts of time and energy on our child's learning and fun.

Thank goodness for love. Though there are challenging moments when we don't know what to do or how to respond to the immensity of children's needs, we do it. Our deep love and appreciation for them carries us through the rough spots.

B.C. – we never imagined how intense our love could be. Now, we would move mountains for them. Yes, we worry. We wonder what will become of these bundles of potential. Then, miraculously, because of us *and* in spite of us, children survive – even thrive!

Yes, our priorities have shifted. We are changed forever by love!

Creative Problem Solving FEBRUARY 3

When a child's behavior demands a reasonable reaction from us, are we prepared to respond appropriately? Or do we say or do the first thing that comes to mind? When we respond without thinking, we are much more likely to regret our reaction.

One of the most important first steps we can take is to remain calm and pause *before* we act. We can let children know that we are going to think before we respond.

> "I'm feeling frustrated. I need a few minutes to
> think about what we should do about this."

In those few moments, ask yourself some important questions:

> *Why does this behavior bother me right now?*
> *What does this behavior say about what this*
> *child needs?*
> *Whose problem is this – Mine? Child's? Both?*
> *What is the best way to deal with this now?*
> *What can be done to prevent this from*
> *happening again?*

We can deal with children's inappropriate behavior in thoughtful, positive ways.

Why Does This Behavior Bother Me?

You name the behavior. One child refuses to do the assigned chore. Another is whining and fussing about having to get dressed for school. Your teen has a snappy comeback to your request that there will be no more video games until homework is done.

Our reaction to these behaviors can vary significantly. The same behavior can trigger a very different reaction depending upon how we are feeling in the moment.

> *Are you stressed after a long, tiring day?*
> *Does it feel like every interaction is a fight?*
> *Are you feeling overwhelmed by today's long list?*
> *Are you feeling rested after a relaxing afternoon?*
> *Are you content, feeling a sense of accomplishment?*

When we are triggered by misbehavior, we can either react with a comeback or we can take a breath and consider our response. Our reaction is the only real place where we have some power. We *can* control how we respond. When we respond with anger, a child's anger is often ignited as well. Then the fight is on. If our reaction is patient, children are more likely to chill out as well.

Recharging Your Batteries

What energizes you? What renews your spirit? This is different for everyone. When a battery loses its charge, it can stop running at any point. You come out of the store, ready to take the groceries home, and your car won't start. We are stranded, sometimes a long way from home. Our own "battery" works much the same way. If we are not doing enough to re-energize our spirit, we run out of steam.

Our bodies tell a pretty accurate story. Tension, fatigue, and stress show up there. Listen to your body. Eat when you are hungry. Drink plenty of water. Stretch and exercise regularly. Rest when you are weary. Sleep when you are tired. BREATHE!!! These basic needs require our attention.

Once our needs are met, we have the energy to ask – "What do I really enjoy?" Identify your pleasures, and then do something fun – read, walk, play music, take a hot bath, or go to a movie.

We need to recharge our batteries. Children need adults who have the energy and patience to pay attention to them.

Walking in a Child's Shoes   FEBRUARY 6

Your child has been fooling around and has just broken a precious memento that belonged to your grandmother. Or, it's bed time and this is the sixth time he has requested something else. Some kind of adult response is called for. A consequence may be needed. What we say and how we respond matters.

Before you respond, ask yourself, "How would I feel if I was a child in this situation? What kind of parental response would be most helpful or supportive right now?" When children occasionally make poor choices, they rarely respond well to a "talking to." A few well-chosen words can be more effective:

> "I know you are aware of our family rule about that. What you did was not okay. I need you to stop what you're doing right now."

How would we feel? We do not want to endure a lecture when we have made a mistake in judgment. Neither do children. We all want to figure this out and move on.

Who's in Control Here?   FEBRUARY 7

We all want to feel we are in control, at least some of the time. So we need to learn how to use our personal power appropriately. When the current situation feels out of control, we feel powerless. We are at a loss for what to do. We would like to get ready and out on time or have chores completed cooperatively or enjoy quiet moments together.

We won't be able to effectively manage frustrating times until we get *ourselves* under control first! Respond calmly. When a child has an angry comeback to your request, don't take the bait. With a reasonable voice, explain the choices:

> "I can tell you are feeling frustrated. Me, too. I
> want us to work together. Right now you have
> two choices. We can do this or that."

Children resist. It's in their job description. They want to be in charge of their lives. We can offer choices that give both of us a sense of control. We can figure out how to share the power. This allows us both to win.

Testing, 1-2-3!   February 8

At all ages, children test. They are checking to see if we will set the limits and follow through with what we have said.

A young, newly walking toddler will go right up to the television and reach for the buttons and knobs, grinning and watching us the whole time. What will our response be? If our face reflects a definitive expression which says, "That's not for you!" then usually the child will back off. It's like this mischievous child is saying, "Are you going to set limits for me? I dare you! Show me who's boss."

Preschoolers test us when they resist routines. School-aged children test, too. Are we really going to insist that they sit down and do their homework? Teens test when they want to stay out with friends beyond our agreed upon curfew.

It is their job to test. Their testing gives us clues about what the child knows and what the child is ready to learn next. Then it is our job to set reasonable limits. As children get older, they demonstrate their ability to make decisions. When we have noticed their readiness to respond with maturity and independence, we can offer new choices.

Your child is resisting something that you believe is good for him.

You must decide who will provide the best care for your child.

Other parents are letting their children participate in something that you don't believe is appropriate.

When a new challenge first surfaces, we don't always know what's best. Sometimes there are too many options. Other times we may feel we don't have enough information. There may be many things to consider –

What does my child need right now?
What is the healthy thing to do in this
situation?
How do I know what's fair for each child?

At these times, we can call upon our inner wisdom to help us reach a hard decision. Inner wisdom comes from the knowledge that we have about children. We also bring previous experiences to the decisions we make. And then we "trust our gut."

When we focus on children's needs and temperament, we consider – "What is really best for this child right now?" Our inner wisdom puts children first!

Rules Are Important FEBRUARY 10

Children need rules. Rules give them a sense of security and safety. They know what to expect and how people will respond to their behavior.

The most effective rules are phrased in terms of what is acceptable. If adults emphasize "Don't..." or "No...", children hear what is *not* okay. "Don't run!" The child still hears "run." They often have a one track mind and need help seeing the acceptable alternative: "Please walk in the store."

All important rules can be understood with two primary

concepts – RESPECT and SAFETY. This simplifies the rules and makes them easier for children to remember. Adults are role models in all situations, so children learn best when we use the same acceptable behavior. Some examples of positively phrased rules are:

> Play calmly inside.
> Cooperate with family members and friends.
> Show kindness and respect in what you say
>   and do.
> Let people know where we are and when we
>   will return.

Children need rules and limits to help shape their behavior. We can provide simple, respectful rules that let children know what is acceptable and what we expect of them.

Let's Talk

No one likes conflict. We want our relationships to run smoothly. But conflicts are a natural part of any relationship – with children, our partner, our friends. When a conflict occurs, it is important to share our feelings and thoughts in order to understand each other and resolve the issue.

When we have a disagreement with someone, hurt feelings can get in the way of resolution. We may even be so angry that we leave and avoid further discussion. When we don't talk about it together, we may imagine the other person's intentions and make assumptions about what was meant. Hurt, disappointment, frustration, and fear can increase.

Effective communication takes *commitment* and time to talk together and really listen to each other. It also takes *honesty* to own up to our feelings. "I was really hurt by your comments." It takes *courage* to admit our mistakes. "I'm sorry. I really regret what I said. I did not mean to hurt you." It also takes *patience* to listen and really hear the other person's point of view.

We can strengthen our relationships by communicating honestly and openly.

Caught Not Taught

Many things that children eventually learn are not taught in a traditional sense, with a lesson and quiet attention to every word delivered by the teacher. Children are paying attention to everything we say and do. They learn by doing – exploring, experimenting, and observing. They watch and listen, and through trial and error, eventually figure it out. They can "catch" an attitude, belief, or value, like we catch a cold, whether we want them to – or not – from exposure.

For example, a parent who has never been comfortable with swimming does not have to pass on this fear of the water. If the parent shows fear, the child may "catch" it, too. Instead, if the child is encouraged to take swimming lessons and the parent watches enthusiastically from the sidelines, the child may never even be aware of the parent's fears. The child can "catch" a love of the water from a parent's encouragement.

When adults demonstrate hatred or prejudice, children often "catch" this attitude, too. Values, behaviors, and attitudes are caught, not just taught. Children are watching and listening, even when we think they are not paying attention.

Discipline Styles Differ

There are many different ways to respond to children's behavior. Some adults keep a very tight rein on children and apply strict punishment when they are "out of line." Some are more permissive or inconsistent, allowing children to do whatever they want. Others communicate openly with them, offering choices, and negotiating conflicts.

When a friend's discipline style clashes with ours, we may find it awkward to spend time together. Maybe your friend yells a lot and is too strict. Or maybe her children's behaviors reflect the fact that she seems to have no rules. When our styles conflict, we may have reservations about allowing the children to play together.

As our children get older and experience other people's

family life, they notice that families are not the same. But, children are adaptable. They learn that parents have different expectations. There are different ways to establish routines. There are different ways to make decisions.

Parents in the same family help their children learn what to expect when they work hard to support each other's style.

All You Need Is Love   FEBRUARY 14

Love does make a difference. We all appreciate hearing words of support or affirmation from people we care about. This communicates, "You are my special girl."

When we have genuine love at the foundation of our interactions, we can endure many things. When children feel loved, they find it easier to understand our expectations. They know that we want the best for them. When love is at the center, even deep hurts can be healed. We forgive.

We show our love in many ways, communicated in our words and our actions. We offer children loving limits when we are clear about what is acceptable and what is not. We demonstrate loving understanding when we are patient and take the time to listen without interruptions. Children feel our love when we tenderly touch their shoulder or give them a hug, for no particular reason.

Love isn't all we need, but feeling loved certainly can have a major influence on how we respond to each day.

Super Kid   FEBRUARY 15

Some schools have a student recognition program that acknowledges children who have done something special in the last week. They may have shown improvement in school work or a noticeable increase in their effort. They may have shown kindness toward another student or helpfulness in the classroom. The goal is for every child to receive this award at least once during the year.

Some children earn this notice quickly and easily. Others

require more effort on the part of adults to identify their behavior from a place of strengths and improvements. We can remember to let children know that we notice:

> "Thanks for helping with the dishes."
>
> "Good for you. You really focused on your homework."
>
> "Your little brother really likes playing with you."
>
> "Even though you were frustrated, you stayed calm."

All children deserve to feel like super kids!

Use Your Words   February 16

We rely on words. Verbal communication is an important part of our interactions. We let people know what we need and want. We can handle our hassles with words. We also learn about each other.

> "How are you feeling?"
>
> "What do you need?"
>
> "Tell me what you like."
>
> "What would help you feel more comfortable right now?"

When children are frustrated or annoyed, their whole body says so. Body language can be misinterpreted. We don't want them to lash out physically and hurt each other. We want them to learn to use words to describe their feelings. Words help us express our love and settle arguments.

> "I'm mad. I don't like it when you do that."
>
> "I don't want to play that right now."
>
> "Hey, I had that first."

Words can hurt. Words can help. We can help children learn to use words to communicate feelings and needs.

An Ounce of Prevention

Not all misbehavior can be prevented. Not all temper tantrums can be avoided. Not all testing of the limits can be stopped. But, we can take steps that help to minimize children's challenging behaviors.

Probably the most important first step is *knowing the child*. When we observe a child, we pick up clues from the behavior. We begin to better understand what this child needs. We see this child's strengths. Then, we can create more realistic expectations.

Everyone is assisted by *knowing the plan*. When we don't know what is coming next, we can be uncomfortably thrown off balance. When we describe our schedule, children are better able to follow through and so are we.

Knowing what to expect helps children realize that they can count on us. They know the rules and they know how we will respond – fairly and consistently.

Knowing what to do helps to prevent hassles. When we plan ahead, we bring activities that will help entertain the child as we wait for an appointment. Children can cope more easily when they have something to do.

Some things will still happen without warning. But, we are better prepared to handle surprises when we plan ahead.

The Little Red Hen

Remember the childhood story of the Little Red Hen? She baked some bread. At every step, she asked for help, and at every step, all those she asked said "no." Then, when the smell of hot, freshly baked bread came floating out of the kitchen, everyone wanted some. This sounds like typical family life. It can be difficult to get help when there is work to be done. But everyone rushes to be first in line when the fun is served out.

This children's story gives us some reminders about family life: Family life includes many responsibilities and demands. We are all asked to participate by sharing the work. There are rewards for helpfulness. When the work is done, we have time to play.

The Little Red Hen was patient and persistent. She continued to ask and offer opportunities to contribute. And in the end, she didn't get mad. She just let those who did not help out experience their own consequences. We teach children everyday by setting an example of commitment, cooperation, and consistency.

Separation Anxiety   FEBRUARY 19

Separation anxiety comes in many forms. In addition to the typical separation issues which happen during the toddler years, traumatic experiences can also increase a child's sense of anxiety – illness, accidents, losses, moving.

Infants and young toddlers eventually realize that their parents are not an extension of their own bodies. So when parents disappear and leave them with a sitter, gone is gone. This can feel pretty scary at first. They do not have a sense of time, but they are relieved when parents return.

As they get older, some children are fearful of new experiences. When there are too many transitions and not enough time to get used to them all, children can feel overwhelmed. We can help them adjust to normal separations by showing patience and acceptance. We can acknowledge their feelings.

> "I know this is hard for you right now. You will
> have a chance to play. I will be back soon."

We can reassure children that we will think about them and love them, even when we are not together.

Hard Times – Happen   FEBRUARY 20

> A loss in the family
> The death of a pet
> A move to a new community
> Divorce

A challenging school year

Hard times happen. We can't avoid them. But, we can try to handle them in healthy ways.

Children do not need all of the details when we are going through hard times. They do need our support. When we are experiencing major challenges, it often shows in our behavior. We have less patience. Our temper is on a short fuse. We aren't sleeping well. We have much less energy. Is it any wonder that our reactions are sometimes reflected in the children's behavior as well?

So, during hard times, it is even more important than usual to slow down, keep consistent routines, offer our love and support, and allow plenty of time for cuddling. We will all get through this much better when we take care of ourselves and each other.

Step by Step   FEBRUARY 21

It seems to happen overnight when a new behavior or skill magically appears. But learning is actually the result of many tiny practice steps.

Reading starts with being read to. Eventually children notice letters and sounds. They see signs in the neighborhood. They begin to sound out the letters, until the magical moment when they get it! Almost like an explosion, they are reading!

Riding a bike starts with noticing bicycles. A tricycle helps with learning to balance. When ready, training wheels can make the dream possible. One day, the world opens up. "Hey, look! No hands!"

We support children in their learning with our patience and our presence. We can read to them. We steady them while they practice balancing.

Social skills are also learned step by step. Communication, manners, politeness, listening, sharing, being a friend. Learning happens in steps with support along the way.

Shopping with Children FEBRUARY 22

Shopping is often a difficult experience for children as well as for adults. Getting in and out of the car four times for four different errands is not fun for them either.

The best way to avoid shopping hassles is to leave children at home. But since this is not always possible, we can help children learn how to behave in public. We can figure out ways to make shopping more fun for everyone.

Timing is important. Remember to schedule the shopping trip when children are rested and fed. We can include children in *planning* for our shopping adventure. We can *talk together* about where we will be going and what we need. When possible, children can choose. "Should we get this cereal or that one?"

Shopping with children does not have to be a trying experience. We can make it fun. Be silly, talk together, sing, laugh together, and play as you go through the aisles.

Advice FEBRUARY 23

Everyone has an opinion. Everyone thinks they have the right solution to our dilemma. Maybe this is not a problem for you, but someone else might think it is!

Unsolicited advice comes from many directions – family, friends, and even complete strangers. Sometimes we appreciate the information. But, we may not. If the advice makes us feel incapable and small, we may respond with resentment.

Or, we can choose to consider the genuine good intentions and respond respectfully:

> "I appreciate your interest. We have put a lot of
> thought into this already, and decided this way
> is best for our family."
>
> Or
>
> "Thank you for the suggestion. I'll think about
> it."

We can respond respectfully to advice, whether solicited or not.

Finding Their Own Way

Some children are born independent. From the time they are toddling around, they are asserting their will on the world. They have something to say! We even find ourselves asking, "Who's really in charge here?" Other children go along with whatever is planned for them. They prefer it when we do things *for* them.

For either child, we can encourage self-reliance. They learn to think and act for themselves when we offer choices. We give them chores so they can eventually take care of themselves on their own. A small allowance helps them deal with money issues. They can walk to school, when it is nearby.

As hard as this is, there will also be times when we must stand by while they fall. We are available for support along the way. And they eventually learn to get back up and decide where to go from here.

Even when we encourage independence, we occasionally have a hard time with some of the decisions that children make on their own. If we hover over them, this says, "I really don't trust that you can handle this. I am worried you'll fall and get hurt."

Children learn best from their *own* efforts, their *own* mistakes, their *own* lessons, their *own* successes. Children eventually find their *own* way in the world.

Fussy Eater

Most children have food favorites and food dislikes. Some children are very particular in their food preferences. This is one of those areas where it is best to "choose your battles." When we fight with kids about issues involving food, we usually lose and mealtimes become a battleground. Food is necessary and tastes are very individual.

Most children outgrow the extremes of their younger years. Yes, they have preferences. So do we. Some foods just don't taste good to them. We can understand this since we generally only prepare those foods which we enjoy.

There are things we can do to insure children are eating enough. We can ask – Is she growing? Does he seem energetic, satisfied, and healthy? We can offer more frequent snacks and try to balance their food intake this way. Children need to eat more often than adults anyway, since they are usually far more active than we are.

We can help them learn to accept a wider variety of foods by offering different textures and tastes. Sometimes children are too busy to sit long for a meal, so forcing them to remain at the table can make mealtime uncomfortable for everyone.

Eating together is so much nicer when it is a pleasant, social experience.

Acting As If   FEBRUARY 26

When we are in the middle of a change, we are sometimes frustrated if things don't move quickly enough. Just like our children on a long car trip, we wonder, "Are we there yet?" We want to be there now!

Sometimes we realize that we need to make a change in the way we are handling children's behaviors. Our same old ways just haven't been working. Children continue to push and test. There must be a better way!

While we are learning new behaviors and habits ourselves, we can "act as if." To do this, we must first stop and think before responding. Then we say to ourselves, "What would I do or say now if I believed I really knew what I was doing and what I wanted?" This puts us in a positive frame of mind to try something new! Affirmations can also help make the shift.

> I can respond in a healthy way.
> I believe I can do this.
> I will beat this depression.

Sometimes when we are in the middle of learning new things, we just have to "do it" and "act as if" we were already there. Then, before we now it, we are!

Pass It On!

We pass on our values and beliefs to children with everything we say and do. Our values are those things that are very important to us. What do we really care about? We also have beliefs that guide us, like:

> Family time is precious.
> Education is important.
> You can do it!
> Children need love and guidance.
> We all share home responsibilities here.

We pass on our values and beliefs in conversation. But, even more importantly, children learn through observation. They watch us. They listen to our words and hear the feelings behind the words.

If we want children to learn to be respectful of others, we must demonstrate respect in what we say and do. Children are more likely to value education when we create a positive atmosphere for learning. Children who become responsible adults have often been encouraged to share the load and cooperate at home and at school. We can give clear messages that communicate our values and beliefs.

Leaving an Impression

As adults, we realize that the only person we can really change is our self. Other people can influence us, but we are the one who decides how we will react and respond in any given situation. When children are young, we have a powerful influence on them. We don't know what the long range outcome will be or who this child will become. This is a big responsibility for us. We must consider the long term effects of our behavior or reactions on their future self-esteem.

What messages do you carry from childhood that are difficult to shake off?

> "How many times have I told you?"
> "When are you going to learn?"

"You did it again! What's wrong with you?"

The choice is ours. We can decide today to give positive impressions –

"I believe in you."

"You are amazing."

"You are learning so much!"

Leap Day   FEBRUARY 29

Today is a bonus. It only comes every four years. In case you didn't realize it, the Earth actually takes about 365.25 days to go around the Sun. So, in order to make the year agree with the course of the Sun, every fourth year, we have to add a day to make up the difference. Today is that special extra day!

This is a day to look back at how far we've come. Then, we can figure out where we want to leap next. We can notice how our child has grown in the last year. The seasons change, and we do, too. Sometimes we get out of sync with each other. Here are some questions to ask yourself:

What new accomplishments have we seen in recent weeks?

What is going well?

What may have gotten off track?

No matter where we are now, we can stop and look at where we've been and what lies ahead. And then we can celebrate our leaps and bounds!

March

No Matter What

One of the gifts we offer children is unconditional acceptance. "You are special to me, no matter what!" When we convey this message, children understand that no matter what they say or do, our love does not go away. We accept them just as they are, with their unique talents and yes, flaws.

We need to separate their behavior from who they are as a person. Each child is loveable and capable. But, sometimes this loving, capable child makes an inappropriate choice. We do not like the behavior that results. Regardless of this, we still accept the child.

Though we want children to feel accepted, the message is not easily received. What is "heard" does not always reflect what we really feel. Sometimes children believe we intended a different message – "I love you *only* when you clean up your room." Or "I accept you *when* you remember to be kind."

We want them to know deep inside that *no matter what*, there is nothing they could ever do that would keep us from loving them.

Doing It with Style

Each child has a unique style called temperament. Some components of temperament include: intensity, mood, persistence, focus, reaction to people and situations, reactions to change, activity level, and sensitivity. A child's style is both inborn and influenced by family life and social experiences.

Some children are comfortable just about anywhere. Some children are loud and excitable, while others are quiet and mellow. Some children can focus for a long time on an activity, while others rarely finish a task. Sometimes children get along easily, while others fight constantly.

When we understand and accept each other's different styles, it feels like a good fit between adults and children. At other times, we wonder, "Where did this child come from?"

We advocate for children when we reframe negative perceptions into strengths. We can help children build their skills and use their unique gifts to find their place in the world.

The next several essays will look at different children, describing their temperaments, their challenges, and their strengths. There will also be ideas on how to best support them and help them be the most they can be. We can learn to accept and appreciate each child's unique style.

Watch and Wait March 3

Waiting on the sidelines, he notices everything, missing none of the details. He is cautious about stepping into a new situation and checks it out before entering. Even then, he will only join in once he has become familiar with the environment and the people. Though he may be slow to warm up to a new setting, when he is ready, he usually has clear, thoroughly thought out ideas.

This child may be a visual learner. He likes to watch it being done, then he can do it. He often prefers playing alone. Or he enjoys being in the background, doing what he can to help make things happen.

Many think of this child as shy and withdrawn. This unfortunate characterization overlooks the potential insights derived from careful observation and attention to detail. If we try to push this child into experiences he is not ready for, he will become very frustrated and may even withdraw further into the shadows.

This child needs to watch and wait. When he is ready, or when the time is right, he will move forward. We can patiently wait, too.

Jumping Right In! March 4

Whenever a new experience presents itself, this child eagerly jumps right in! Quick to explore, she shows no hesitation. In fact, she may be hard to rein in. If we try to hold her back, she can become very impatient and frustrated. She approaches each new situation with curiosity and excitement.

Our concern is that her curiosity may get the best of her. Since she is often fearless and may not think before acting, she might get hurt or into trouble. Her impulsive responses sometimes lead to unhealthy or dangerous choices.

The same impulsive behavior is also part of her charm. She can be the life of the party and is ready to have fun! She can be creative and quick to discover new possibilities. She seems to embrace life for everything it is worth.

How can we support this child's eagerness and zest for life *and* provide sufficient safeguards? We can give her lots of space, offer choices, and provide opportunities for adventure. And when needed, we can be right there to share the fun.

The Princess and the Pea   MARCH 5

In this childhood fairy tale, a prince is looking for a real princess. He puts all of the willing Princess-wannabes to the test. He believes that a real princess is sensitive and would feel a pea, even when it is under many layers of mattresses.

There are many such princes and princesses who are touchy and sensitive, including adults.

> They are irritated by the tags in their shirts.
> If there is lint in a sock, off come the sock and
>   shoe with howls of discomfort!
> Any noise at bedtime, and she just can't sleep.
> He doesn't like to be touched, unless he initi-
>   ates or you ask permission, "Can I have a
>   hug?"
> As an extremely picky eater, many foods "taste
>   funny" and are unacceptable.
> This child is easily overstimulated by bright
>   lights and busy settings.

These sensory experiences are truly difficult for some children. They do not react dramatically just to irritate us. Even though this behavior can try our patience, our understanding helps them ask for what is needed – soft clothes, calm sounds, subtle lighting. Once we understand, we can help them feel more comfortable. Then, a world of sights and sounds can open up to these children.

Busy Body MARCH 6

Some children are born with their movement switch stuck in the "on" position. Even when they are sleeping, they move all over the bed. They motion dramatically when they talk and mimic the body language and gestures of others. They get into trouble for touching or becoming too rough during play. They can also be very affectionate, knocking us over with an enthusiastic hug! Their bodies speak volumes. It is unrealistic to expect them to sit still.

What *is* reasonable is to give alternative behavior choices that include appropriate outlets for their energy. "You are spinning around with lots of energy right now. Let's go outside and throw the ball together."

Busy children enjoy engaging in sports or active play. They prefer activities in short time blocks to maximize their attention. Learning can be enhanced when this child is encouraged to use his whole body. For example, when doing math calculations, it may help him to jump the numbers or manipulate blocks.

This child needs lots of room to move. With just a little encouragement, the active child can also be very physically fit.

In a Mood MARCH 7

Oh, she's in a mood today. Ever since she woke up, she has been grumpy about everything. When you offer a reasonable choice, she says, "No way!" We all have good days and bad days. Good days are great. During bad days, nothing seems to go right. Every turn can lead to another sticky situation. Watch out if your child is feeling frustrated, too.

Some people are more serious about everything. They are perceived as slow to warm up to new people or situations. People often mistake their serious expressions for sadness or anger. Their laughter is more subtle, but they enjoy a good joke. Others have a sunny disposition and are often smiling. They see the best in people. Even after a very challenging experience, they have a way of looking on the bright side.

No matter what someone else's mood might be, we don't have to let it influence our own. We can give children the tools to turn grumpy into gleeful. We can teach them to lighten up and not take some things so seriously.

Drama Queen (or King) MARCH 8

Everything she says or does is high intensity and high volume. Feelings are never a mystery as she expresses her enthusiasm by screeching with joy. Or, when he is upset about something, he rages through the house throwing things and kicking whatever is in his path.

This child enjoys attention and lives on the extremes, either very excited or bitterly disappointed. At least their feelings are clear at any given moment.

We may feel drawn into the drama. We must caution ourselves to remain calm in this atmosphere of frenzy. Joining in with our own intense reactions only adds fuel to an already fiery encounter. Our patience can help to cool down this child's fury. We can help redirect their need to be on center stage as they learn to work cooperatively.

The same intensity that can be frustrating during a power struggle can be an asset as a leader. The ability to take command and delegate tasks can help get the job done. This child has a zest for life that we don't want to stifle.

Staying on Task MARCH 9

Some children have a hard time paying attention and staying on task. All children have their own unique wiring. Some are very organized and careful. Others are very active. Some are joyful and always seem to cheerfully view the world. They easily engage socially and may find it challenging to focus on solo tasks.

We can help children with their focus skills by noticing what they are doing before interrupting with a request. We can make our requests simple, with one or two steps. We can offer to work together, so we can help them stay on task. We can also give positive feedback when the task is done.

Many adults who had a difficult time focusing as a child have learned how to manage tasks today. Most of us can focus on an activity for 15 minutes. We can help children learn to stay on task, too.

Impulse Control   MARCH 10

Are you able to resist warm chocolate chip cookies right out of the oven? Do you always think before speaking? Or do you sometimes regret what you just said or did and wish you could take it back?

There are two distinct sides to impulsive behavior. Some impulsive actions lead to trouble. Or it may be hard to stay focused if something else attracts our attention. Though we often think of impulsive behavior as troublesome, it isn't always. Some people are quick to laugh and quick to act. They don't always need lots of time to decide when something is right. Off they go to the next exciting adventure.

Impulse control is a challenge for everyone at least some of the time, and for children, often! Impulsiveness can be problematic. Impulsiveness can also be a gift when it leads to creativity and healthy fun.

Over time, children learn to wait. They learn to ask first. They learn to think before acting. But, hopefully, they also retain eagerness to try new things, and just do it because it feels right!

Stubbornness Takes Two   MARCH 11

"This child is SO stubborn!
She fights at every turn!"

Yes, children sometimes resist our attempts to direct their

behavior. They want to do it their way. If asked, children might say that WE are the stubborn ones because we want them to do it OUR way. You won't allow her to stay up and watch TV until 10 p.m., even if her homework is done. This is just too late.

So, how can we approach children in an attitude of cooperation and negotiation? How can we reach a compromise that works for us both? Surely, this process of give and take will be translated into future adult life skills.

The first step is to acknowledge the child's feelings. "I know you are feeling frustrated about this right now." This kind of response often takes the wind out of resistant sails, resulting in a willing attitude of negotiation.

Then, we can calmly continue to make peace and mediate the issue. "I understand that you would really like to do that, but we are doing this first. How about you spend 15 minutes on this, and then you will have some time for your own activity?"

Since stubbornness takes two, the person we have the most power to influence is our self. We can choose our battles wisely. We can respond patiently and find a compromise that will be acceptable for both of us.

Chaos Magnet MARCH 12

Maybe it's just a developmental stage. Or an on-going reflection of an intense temperament. Some children just seem to attract chaos. They feel like a victim. Everything seems to happen to them, and they let us know it! If you live with this, you've heard it all!

"No one likes me!"

"I never get ice cream after school!"

"You promised!"

"It's his fault! I didn't get a turn!"

Though this behavior is frustrating to us, think about how painful it must be for the child. This is a child who is often hurting. We can help with our patience and understanding.

Don't get triggered by this dramatic reaction. We need to be careful not to be sucked into taking care of it and fixing it. With our help, this child can learn to cope. We can acknowledge feelings, "I can tell this is very frustrating for you." Children can learn the social skills needed to deal with tough times.

We can also reframe our understanding of this behavior and find the strengths. These same children often show great enthusiasm. When they find something they enjoy, they are very excited. When they care, they care deeply. They let us know what they are thinking and feeling, so there are no surprises.

We can learn to respond calmly and appreciate this child's sensitivity and enthusiasm for life.

Spirited Children   MARCH 13

A spirited child is a feisty child who often reacts intensely. She may also be a shy child who is uncomfortable in groups. Some spirited children are energetic and have one speed setting: "on." He may also be an inquisitive child who talks non-stop and asks endless questions. This child has spirit!

These children can also be a challenge to themselves and others. Our role is to help them figure out how to deal with life's struggles in their own unique way.

Children thrive when they feel loved and accepted just as they are. We can provide the comfort of routines which help them know what to expect. We can teach them coping and social skills. Sometimes we also need to protect them from people who have unreasonable expectations. Spirited children realize there is something different about them. We can support their unique style.

What Are My Child's Strengths?   MARCH 14

Children have many strengths. We don't always see them. Sometimes we are frustrated. So are they. They are whiny and irritable. They are overwhelmed. They are unwilling to listen. The same can sometimes be said of us.

But, certainly, when we want to work something out, the power to find a solution is in recognizing the strengths. Some strengths are listed below. Start by noticing the strengths, then tell your child. Opportunities will open quickly.

appreciative	energetic	motivated
assertive	focused	negotiator
beautiful	friendly	patient
bold	funny	playful
bright	generous	respectful
capable	giving	responsible
careful	grateful	safe
compassionate	helpful	sensitive
confident	honest	strong
considerate	intelligent	supportive
creative	learning	thoughtful
determined	listener	unique
eager	loveable	wise

Light at the End of the Tunnel MARCH 15

When we are going through a challenging time, it may seem like it will never end. Every day is so difficult.

We can learn to look at this experience in a different way. Rather than allowing ourselves to be swallowed up by frustrations, we can look for hints that change is occurring and adjustments are being made. The light of resolution is beginning to flicker on the edges.

Some children have an especially difficult time adjusting to new situations. We call this child "slow to warm up." Whether this is the first day of school or a new neighbor has moved in nearby, this child's comfortable, secure routines are thrown off. After an uneasy period, balance slowly begins to reestablish itself. There is less clinging and greater confidence. She is smiling more and has an easier time connecting with others.

The signs are there. We can see the light at the end of this tunnel. It rarely helps to push children through these periods. They must move at their own pace. But, we can offer encouragement.

> "I know new things are hard for you, but I can tell you are getting a little more comfortable. Let me know if there is anything I can do to help."

Getting What We Expect   MARCH 16

Some assumptions can be like magic. If we assume our child will be naughty and disobedient, he often is. This is the classic "self-fulfilling prophecy."

But, like magic, when we assume the best, we are often pleasantly surprised by the wonderful things children do to prove it to us.

> "You're a hard worker. You want to get this done so you can move on to another activity."

When we expect the best, as long as these expectations are reasonable and realistic, we are often rewarded with helpful, cooperative behavior. And children feel acknowledged by our positive response:

> "Look at that, you did it! You finished in time."

We often get what we expect, so expect well!

Don't Take It Personally   MARCH 17

> "I hate you!"
> "I'm never going to be your friend again!"
> "You never understand!"

In these intense moments of anger and frustration, children lash out at us. We may feel like issuing a comeback with a biting reaction, "Don't you dare talk to me that way!!"

But, it is so much better to respond with understanding. Acknowledge the feelings and let go of any thought that your child really means this. We all exaggerate sometimes. We can also keep our response simple and do our best to restore good feelings.

"I know you are really disappointed right now.
I just want you to know that I am here for you.
When you are ready, let's talk about this."

Children are reassured to know that adults can handle strong feelings without retaliating. We don't have to take it personally.

Breathe! You're Out of the Storm   MARCH 18

You've just come out of a very difficult week...or month. Your child seems to have picked up on your feelings of being overwhelmed. She has been demonstrating her own frustrations and demands at every turn.

But not today. You hardly recognize her. She is sweet, pleasant, attentive, agreeable. All smiles. You ask her to help and she cheerfully agrees. You find yourself holding your breath – "Is this my child?"

Sometimes, right before a growth spurt or a significant new ability emerges, children go through a rocky period. They are fussy and disagreeable. Then overnight, they have reached a new milestone and our sunny child is back.

The same thing can happen to us. We go through rough periods, too. Our child may even be thinking, "What is wrong?" And then, we work through the difficulty and come out on the sunny side.

Breathe! Be patient. Hard times come and go. It's going to be okay.

Happy Birthday   MARCH 19

Birthdays mark the anniversary of a child's birth. On birthdays we also recall when we first became parents. Do you remember the day your child was born? Was it scary? Exciting? Exhausting? Was the birth an easy one, or was the process long and difficult? What was it like when you first saw your child? Or, if your child is adopted, the first time you held her is stamped into your memory.

We feel awed and amazed once our child is put into our arms. It becomes difficult to imagine our lives without them. Many possibilities lie ahead.

Birthdays are a time to celebrate life. Some families have big parties, while others have a quiet, more intimate gathering. No matter how we honor the day, we want to let children know that this is their special day. We are glad they came to live with us. Birthdays are a good day to share our memories.

Hero Worship   MARCH 20

What does it take to be a hero to a child? Children need someone to look up to. They need someone who is capable of showing them the way. They need someone who is powerful enough to protect them from the "bad guys." Children need someone who can do the things they can't but wish they could.

Who were the heroes in your life? Was it a grandfather who was successful in spite of a disability? Did you have a single mother who worked hard so you and your siblings could have what you needed?

Sometimes children pick heroes who are not such good role models – rock stars and celebrities, video game or cartoon characters, older children in the neighborhood who are popular but take unsafe risks.

Children need heroes. They can look for them in books, on the television, or in their neighborhoods. Or, they can find them in their own homes.

Spring is Here!   MARCH 21

Everywhere we look, we see lush green in the swaying grass, the hint of new life on trees, and all the colors of the rainbow in the wildflowers dotting the hillsides. Gardens are eagerly awaiting our love and care as we prepare the soil for spring plantings and the hope of the eventual harvest. The sky reflects the clear blue of longer daylight and the seasonal rains offer up life-giving potential.

Spring is a time of renewed energy, possibilities and growth. Children also seem to be bursting at their seams with excitement and growth. After the inwardness of winter, it's time to move and explore. It's time to put away the winter coats and encourage children to go outside to enjoy the day. We can keep boots and umbrellas handy for puddle jumping.

Along with the new possibilities of spring, there will be inevitable resistance as well. Each child, just like each flower, has a unique timeline for growth. We can't push the flowers. Children, too, bloom when they are ready.

Enjoy springtime. New experiences are on the way.

Ignoring It! MARCH 22

We pay way too much attention to annoying behaviors. We need to figure out what we can ignore and what is serious enough to warrant our immediate attention. There are annoyances that are not hurtful to people or property: a sassy comeback to our request; busy energy that just doesn't seem to quit; loud voices heard from across the house; or squabbles between children that are not hurtful.

We need to be careful to avoid matching this child's behavior with our own rude reaction. We can respond respectfully. And when possible, we can ignore them. Sometimes ignoring requires an explanation:

> "If you are going to talk that way, I can't help you right now. I am going to the other room. When you can ask me nicely, we'll be able to work it out together."

Or we can watch and wait to see if they are able to work out their hassle peacefully without our help. We don't have to react to everything. Sometimes we can just take a breath and let it go. Is this really such a big deal? Is a response from me really needed right now?

Expect the Unexpected

What can we count on? The sun rises and sets every day. Spring follows Winter. Baby teeth loosen and fall out, and new ones come in. And children grow up, sometimes much faster than we want.

But, things often do not go according to plan, no matter how hard we try to anticipate what's next. So, what can we *really* count on? As soon as we think we have things all figured out, they change.

Be ready to respond to the unexpected. We need to "go with the flow." We can ask ourselves at these times, "What is life trying to teach me right now? What is the lesson I need to learn?" Slow down. Practice patience. And trust that when we do our best, many things do work out.

It really is true that "Life is what happens while you are busy making other plans." So, be ready for the surprises. We can figure out how to sail through the pleasures or the mishaps, remembering that children are learning from our example.

Too Many "Parents"

Sometimes children have too many "parents"– mom, dad, a big sister, grandparents, child care providers, teachers. It can be confusing to deal with all of the different styles and demands.

Children learn that adults have different perspectives. It's hard for them when adults disagree about which tack to take or which plan is best. We can help them out by agreeing or by letting one adult be in charge at a time. Sometimes in a heated moment, we may ask for a "hand off" of responsibility to allow someone with a more relaxed perspective to take over. Otherwise, we need to be respectful and avoid undermining each other's authority.

Children like to know what to expect. It is difficult for them when they receive mixed messages from the important adults in their lives. Clear, regular communication between adults helps to create consistent expectations and consequences. We can develop open communication channels between ourselves and the other adults in children's lives. We can work together for the best interests of children.

It's How We Say It MARCH 25

There's no avoiding it. Adults need to set limits and children resist them. What makes a difference in our interactions is not so much about the limit we set, but the way we enforce it. It is not so much about what we say, but how we say it.

When our bristly anger comes charging through, children feel frightened and frustrated. They may be immobilized by our anger or tempted to rebel and counter with their own temper and resistance.

We are much more likely to gain a child's cooperation if we ask with a firm, yet even tone of voice. Sometimes it helps to take a few deep breaths. Our energy becomes more focused. We can also give ourselves a positive "talking to" before opening our mouth to speak:

> "Okay, now, go easy. Remember, he's only three
> and you're in charge."

Now we are more prepared to speak with understanding and determination:

> "I know you would rather stay home right now,
> but I need you to put that away so we can leave
> on time."

Our respectful communication is much more likely to get the results we are looking for. We will both feel better.

Friendships MARCH 26

What does it mean to be a friend? When children are young, this is pretty simple. They play together or side by side. As their imagination grows, the interactions intensify and sometimes negotiations are needed to figure out who is going to do what in their play drama.

"You be the kid, and I'll be the teacher."
"No, I want to be the teacher!"
"We can both be teachers."
"Yeah, the dolls can be the kids."

Solid friendships start to develop during the school-age years as children share interests, activities, school events, sports. Good friends often have similar personalities and styles and engage in generally comfortable interactions.

But, learning to be a friend is a process, like so many lessons during childhood. Learning to be a friend means spending time together, practicing give and take, and resolving conflicts.

Some children find it difficult to be a friend. Some children are leaders, while others are easily led. Some want to do everything their own way and have a hard time being flexible. It is helpful when adults are available to walk children through the natural disputes which arise. We can provide a comfortable, supervised environment where friendships can grow.

It's the Little Things That Count MARCH 27

When we look back on our children's childhoods, we will remember the precious moments that passed by in a whisper.

"Thanks, mom."
"You can use my blanket, daddy."
When 3-year-old big brother brought you 1-
    week-old sister, because "She missed you,
    Mom."
Giggles and smiles
"I love you."
A tea party with dolly
A walk in the rain together
Stopping at the park to swing
One more goodnight hug and kiss

His first bike ride, without your help
An unexpected conversation with a teen
"You're so cool, dad!"

These things matter. Not the hassles. Not the frustrations.

Trial and Error MARCH 28

All learning is a result of trial and error. Some things are easier to learn. Others require many errors before we finally get it right! The same is true for parenting. Children do not come with an instruction manual. And even if you had time to read every book on the subject, there are no magic solutions. Each child remains at least partly *a mystery.*

Why is she crying?
What does he need right now?
When will I understand this child?

Over time, we get better at interpreting behavior and feelings. For a brief period, we even seem to be in sync. Then, along comes another major growth spurt, and new mysteries surface. At these times, it may feel like we are starting all over.

But, we continue to learn. We do know our child. We've been through a lot together. With love, patience, and good intentions, we'll get through this, too.

Table Talk MARCH 29

Many have let sitting down together for a family meal slip away. In generations past, this was one of the times when family members would share stories from their day. If this was a "children should be seen and not heard" family, at least the children were able to hear about what was significant in the adults' lives.

It is time to call for a family meal revival. In our busy lives, meal times are an opportunity to meet face to face and connect. We can make meal times fun. Very young children don't always have the patience to wait out the entire meal.

Rather than have their squirmy complaints disrupt this time for everyone, release them from their chair to go play elsewhere.

When children are at the table, we can focus our conversations on topics that will include them. This is not a time for adults to expect to be able to talk together without interruptions. A family meal can be a time to –

Share stories.

Ask questions.

Plan together.

Laugh together.

On Your Own MARCH 30

Whether a single parent full-time, or part-time because a partner works long hours, many parents are often on their own. Without support and parenting assistance, the responsibilities of family life fall primarily on one parent.

Support is always important. We don't feel so isolated when we hear that someone else is dealing with similar issues with their child. We can also ask for help with child care and chores.

During especially stressful times, it helps to simplify routines. What are the most important things to accomplish? How can I be sure to build in plenty of time to interact with my child?

Everyone benefits from alone time, like a twenty minute walk between work and picking up children from child care or school. This gives us a chance to clear our heads of work concerns and prepare to focus on our children.

Raising children on our own is possible. But, we were never meant to shoulder all the responsibility. We can quickly collapse into a serious burnout if we forget to take care of ourselves and reach out for support!

Too often we approach many of our daily experiences way too seriously. We "make mountains out of mole hills." When we are tired or frustrated or overwhelmed, we react to everything with the same intense energy. A minor hassle becomes a major obstacle. Is it really such a big deal? Must I be so serious about this? What would happen if I reacted differently? Can I let this go? Yes, I can lighten up!

> *Lighten up* – Children can be redirected much more easily with a smile and gentle coaxing than with a stern expression and a tense body.

> *Lighten up* – Our attitude can help them feel more open to listening and working with us.

> *Lighten up* – We benefit, too, when our reaction is more relaxed. We experience less stress. Our own health and energy is taxed less when we avoid intense reactions.

> *Lighten up!*

April

Changing the Dance

We have a rhythm with children. We are used to responding to each other in certain ways. Often we keep doing the same thing with them, yet expect a different result. Sometimes consistency eventually gets a new response. But, usually we need to figure out our part of the dance, and change the steps.

Notice the dance steps. Remember that children's steps include testing. They want to get what they want when they want it. We can try some new steps:

Change of Pace – Slow down or do something more active. Sometimes a change of energy shifts the behavior.

Change of Location – Move to another room, from outside to inside, or inside to outside.

Change of Activity – Try a totally different activity. If he has been busy, try something quieter.

Change of Discipline – We need to respond to inappropriate behavior. But, the same discipline does not work with every child, every time.

Change of Attitude – Does my child feel my unconditional love and understanding?

Dancing together requires constant readjustment. We can be out of step or we can try to figure out a way to be in sync. Finding a new rhythm together is possible.

Let's Be Honest About Abuse

April is Child Abuse Prevention Month. Abuse happens. When children are mistreated, there is often a family history of abuse. Or sometimes adults have unrealistic expectations for children's behavior. There is never a time when a child deserves harsh discipline. Firm, loving limits are important. But, intense physical punishment or belittling words are never appropriate.

Many adults who were abused as children have put these

hurtful memories behind them until they become parents themselves. Then, when busy children misbehave, as all children do, memories of our own childhood may resurface. Parents may ask themselves, "How do I deal with my child in a healthy way? I do not have experiences that can help me respond effectively."

Some reminders can help us be more effective –

> The *most effective time-out* is the one the adult takes in the heat of the moment. Take yourself away and calm down so you can respond with patience.
>
> *Get support.* Caring for children is demanding. They do not come with instructions, so talking with someone helps.
>
> *Classes also offer ideas* that help us understand children's behavior and deal with issues in positive ways.

We can learn to "keep our cool" and interact with children with patience and acceptance. Child abuse is preventable. Every child deserves to live with adults who understand them and treat them with love and respect.

Triggered   APRIL 3

> Your children are fighting. Your teen doesn't want to let his younger sister use the video game. After all, he paid for it with his own money.

Listening to children argue is very upsetting. We want them to be generous. We want them to be able to share and cooperate. We can so easily slip into lecture-mode at times like these. Very quickly, we see our teen roll his eyes. After another minute, he turns and leaves the room. Unable to let this go, we follow...and on it goes!

We have been triggered. Maybe this behavior has brought up experiences from our own childhood. Maybe we are exhausted after a long work day. Maybe we're just tired of these hassles between the kids.

Stop! When we are angry, we are not thinking clearly. When we are triggered, we are not likely to create a positive outcome. When a child's behavior sets off something in us, this is exactly the time to take a break. Then, once things have settled down, we can address our concerns.

We can take a breath or take some time to cool down. Now we can address the situation with patience.

Understanding Anger   APRIL 4

Anger usually gets a bad rap. But anger isn't bad. It's what we do with it that gets us into trouble.

Anger is a dramatic signal that something is wrong. When we are angry, there are other feelings underneath. We might be feeling hurt, disappointed, scared, or unappreciated. The trick is to learn to talk about those feelings before they fester into an angry reaction.

When we let our feelings explode out with loud voices and tense bodies, anger gets the upper hand and people get hurt. If instead, we use words to express our feelings, anger is often eased. Children can learn how to deal with their feelings in healthy ways when we demonstrate by using our words.

We can also let children know that everyone gets angry, sometimes. When we say or do something that we regret, an apology is needed. Children are usually ready to forgive. They are also more likely to express their feelings when we set an example.

Choices   APRIL 5

Offering choices gives children a sense of control. When we give "limited" choices, we still have a say in the outcome, but we give children a choice between two or three options.

"Would you like soup or a sandwich?"

"Do you want to do your homework first or

play for 30 minutes before homework?"
"Would you rather ride bikes or play in the
back yard?"

Choices often help settle a disagreement before it expands into a more intense drama.

"I know you would like to do that. But, we only have a few minutes, so you can do this instead."

Sometimes a very bold child will say, "I don't want those choices." If so, the adult can calmly say, "Do you want to choose or do you want me to choose?" Most children will choose for themselves because they want to feel that they are in charge. Offering choices helps us negotiate an agreement. We can both have a say in the situation.

That Trusty Timer

Many of us carry around an internal clock and calendar. We have a sense of time and write our plans in our calendars. We make lists to remember the things we need to do.

Children live in the present. They don't carry our plans in their heads. They have their own ideas for right now. To help them prepare for the next scheduled activity, children need a respectful warning. "In ten more minutes we're going to clean this up so we can go to the store."

We can choose to use a timer. When the timer rings, it is the boss. This external reminder can smooth out conflicts.

"Oh, the timer is telling us it's clean-up time."

Or, when children are having a hard time sharing a toy –

"How about you take a turn for fifteen minutes.
When the timer rings, it will be his turn."

Timers can signal something the child is looking forward to:

"We are going to have a one hour rest period.
When the timer rings, we will play together."

There are many uses for timers. They have a gentle authority that helps things work out in a fair way.

Modify the Environment

Her bedroom looked just the way her mom thought a little girl's room should look. She had a pretty pink bedspread. The dresser was next to the bed and all her stuffed animals rested neatly on top of the dresser. They had a night time ritual of saying goodnight to all those "friends."

But, this little girl was not three yet and she was quite a climber. She loved to get up on her bed and climb onto an open drawer. Then she pushed all the stuffed animals onto the floor, climbed up onto the dresser and jumped gleefully onto the bed.

Well, of course, mom was worried that her daughter might get hurt. This had become a regular battle. No amount of logic worked on this busy little toddler. So, what was mom to do? After talking with some other parents, she realized she needed to change her expectations about what the room looked like. Safety needed to come first.

Move the dresser! She put the dresser on the other side of the room. She put most of the stuffed animals on a high shelf and her daughter picked the ones she wanted to sleep with each night. Getting her to stop jumping on the bed was still a challenge, but since the dresser was gone, the safety issue was not as intense.

Sometimes we need to adjust the environment *and* our expectations a little. And in doing so, a battle is ended.

Explain the Plan

We alone know what we are thinking. We have a vision of what we want. And yet, we expect others to read our minds, anticipate our wishes and "do it" without explanation. This is not realistic. Young children live in the moment and do not have a good sense of time. So, we can let children know what the day looks like. They usually only need a "heads up" on events that will occur that day or very soon.

> "After school, you have soccer. I have a meeting tonight, so let's read together before I go."

Rather than assuming children know exactly what we want, we can spell out the steps. Instead of saying, "Remember to take out the trash," break it into pieces:

> "Get a bag out of the cupboard and go to all the rooms and dump the trash cans. Then, take that bag and the kitchen trash outside to the trash bin. Thank you for your help."

When we clearly communicate our wishes, we are more likely to get what we want.

Consistency   APRIL 9

Consistency helps children learn what adults expect. Consistency tells children they can count on us to follow through when they forget the limits and misbehave.

Consistency does not mean *always* sticking to the same plan, no matter what. As children grow, the discipline response required for misbehavior changes. Appropriate reactions are influenced by the situation. We also consider the child's needs and challenges at this moment. Being consistent with discipline requires some flexibility, depending upon the child, the situation, and the timing.

The most important aspect of consistency is that we will intervene with an appropriate reaction. It is not so important that the same response always follows the same misbehavior. What *is* consistent is that we can be counted on to step in when needed. What *is* consistent is that we care and intend to help the child work through this issue. What may vary is how we decide to deal with this specific situation.

Children thrive on consistent responses that demonstrate our love and commitment at every turn.

How Many Times Do I Have to Tell You?   APRIL 10

Sometimes we are exhausted at the end of the day because of all the times we needed to redirect the children. Children learn over time *with* our reminders. Their curiosity or frustrations can create the motivation to try, risk, study, practice, listen, and learn. Then one day, their new behavior lets us know they finally get it! Now, they are more likely to remember in the future.

When your two-year-old climbs on the back of the couch for the tenth time today, call on your patience. He doesn't realize there are possible consequences or dangers for both himself and the couch. Children don't have the impulse control, especially in times of curiosity or excitement. He is not thinking about the future; he is enjoying now. Remind him again that climbing on the couch is not safe. Distract him by offering another choice.

Be careful not to threaten: "If you do that one more time...." Because he will. And you may feel compelled to respond with a punishment you really don't want to impose. Instead, redirect his activity. Notice his acceptable behaviors and reinforce them: "You're having fun playing safely on the slide!"

So, "How many times do I have to tell you?" One hundred times...*and* at least one more.

The Broken Record APRIL 11

With an old fashioned record player, a scratch could be very annoying. As it played our favorite tune, it got stuck in a scratch. The music repeated, like a hiccup. If we respond to children like a threatening broken record, they sometimes learn to tune us out. "If you don't stop now, I'm going to...."

Children rarely believe this threat, and their repeated behavior pushes us to the breaking point. Maybe we even give in. Instead, we need to remind them once and then be ready to follow through.

> "I'm sorry you can't do that right now. Please put that away. It's nearly dinner time."

There is another kind of broken record that can have a more positive effect. Sometimes children keep coming back for more, to see if we really mean what we just said. They may even nag or whine as they repeat their request. We can reaffirm what we just said by repeating it again, patiently.

"I know this is hard for you, but we aren't going
to do that right now."

Children can get the idea that we mean what we say when we follow through. They learn that no amount of complaining will change our mind on this issue. They need to be able to count on us.

Who's On Our Team?   APRIL 12

We were not meant to care for children alone, isolated from others. We need emotional and physical support. Family life is a big job!

Family members can be on our team. Grandparents can be a big help. They can be role models. They love their grandchildren, no matter what. Our siblings can also help us. But, just because they are relatives doesn't guarantee that they're on our team.

Friends can listen. When we're feeling frustrated, it helps to have someone to talk to. Just saying it out loud often helps us find our own solution.

Other people who care for our children can give us ideas on how to deal with challenging situations. Teachers are important team members. When family members and teachers work together, children are more likely to experience success.

When we are feeling frazzled and worn out, we can't always focus on what is needed right now. Our team can step in to provide the resources we need to get through this next challenge.

Finding a Sitter   APRIL 13

Parents need an evening out. Whether for an important meeting or just for fun, parents need a break.

Some parents realize that, "It takes a village to raise a

child." They have a strong support network that offers assistance whenever needed. Others are more isolated and find it hard to get help.

We are not meant to parent alone. We are social beings and need to connect with others. We can find a sitter who enjoys children and is willing to help us.

> We can ask around and find out who others trust for child care.
>
> We can interview the older children of friends and neighbors to discover who has the maturity and experience.
>
> We can ask someone to come over during the afternoon when we are there, to pay attention to our child so we can pay attention to some other things.
>
> We can trade off with another parent in a cooperative arrangement.

When we take some time away, we feel more refreshed during our time with children.

Just Say "No" April 14

When we want to stop misbehavior, "No!" is rarely enough. Children often have a one track mind. The inappropriate activity has somehow engaged the child's curiosity. Unless we redirect them to a different activity, the behavior is not likely to change.

Children need our help to learn to do the right thing. The unacceptable behavior is much more likely to stop when we offer engaging alternatives.

> "It's not okay for you to get into those shelves and play with those dishes. Climb down. Let's go into your room and find something else for you to do."

Your child wants a cookie. The demanding whine will continue, unless you give a clear explanation.

"No. We are going to eat dinner soon. You can
have a banana if you need a snack."

Children test adults all the time. They want to do what
they want, when they want to do it. Since children don't
always have all of the details, it is our job to explain and let
them know what is acceptable.

The Voice Within   APRIL 15

Most of us have an internal voice that is critical when we
make a mistake.

"You know better than that!"

"How many times are you going to do that before
you remember to avoid the same mistake?"

"That was stupid! What were you thinking?"

These comments may have come from adults or peers
during our growing up years. They never helped us then,
and they don't help children now either. Scolding responses
don't feel good and they don't help us learn. We all make
mistakes. We all occasionally act too quickly or respond
without thinking.

What kind of reactions might be helpful for children to
hear during a frustrating time? When children make a mistake,
we can acknowledge feelings and offer encouragement.

"I know this is disappointing. Would you like
to try again?"

Or if needed, offer assistance.

"That's frustrating. Can I do anything to help?"

Everyone makes mistakes. Encouragement is more likely
to help children move on or try again.

Rainy Day Wiggles   APRIL 16

Dark clouds overhead signal the rain to come. Whether it
is the first rain after a long dry spell or the umpteenth storm
in many days, the weather can be a blessing or a curse. If you

are a sun worshipper, rain is hard anytime. If you love rain and thunder, hooray.

No matter how you feel about the rain, children have their own reactions. We *can* make the most out of this day!

Some children are busy and high energy. If so, it's time to put on boots and raincoats, get out the umbrellas, and enjoy the wet. We can hear the unrestrained glee as children splash through the puddles. Face pointing up, she catches raindrops on her tongue.

When they have had enough of the wet, we can greet them at the door with a warm towel. We can make cookies together, dance to some music, play board games, or draw with big paper.

Rainy days can be wonderful. Are we having fun yet?

Noticing APRIL 17

We are embarrassed when our child fusses and whines in the grocery store.

We are frustrated when our child's teacher says homework hasn't been turned in lately.

We feel overwhelmed when no one is cooperating with chores.

It seems way too easy to notice the misbehavior. We are quick to react with body language and verbal responses that make our feelings very clear.

Sometimes it takes more effort to notice when things are going well. But, we can notice the positive things. She is playing gently with little sister. He brought his dirty dishes to the counter. Homework is finished without a fuss. We can remember to acknowledge these times with a smile, a thumbs-up, or an exclamation of "All right!"

Results are more likely to be positive when we put less reactive energy on some of the misbehavior and decide to notice more of the acceptable behaviors.

Just As You Are

What an incredible message this is – "I love you, just as you are." And how difficult this is to communicate. Too often, children feel there are strings attached. They believe that when their behavior is acceptable, *then* they are acceptable and loveable. But, we want them to really understand that:

> "You are my special boy, just as you are."
> "Even when you scream and fight with your
>   sister, I still love you."
> "I love you, even when you resist sitting down
>   to finish your homework."
> "I love you even though math is a struggle for
>   you."

The message – "Just as you are" – says I accept you as a person...

> With abilities and challenges,
> With strengths and weaknesses,
> Who gets angry and can also be kind,
> And who is learning and growing every day.

One More Chance

When do we give up on children? NEVER!

> "Mom, please give me one more chance. I promise I'll remember to put away my bike."
> "Okay. I am trusting you on this one. I expect you to be responsible and remember to put your bike away. If you don't, I will put it away for several days as a reminder."

This is very different from giving in with a "Whatever!" Children need to know that they can count on us to set reasonable limits for them. They also need to know that pushing us won't get them what they want right now. This is all part of creating a relationship of mutual trust.

The bike was not left out on purpose. Children become distracted. They are busy. Their mind jumps ahead to the next activity. Giving a second chance – one more time – means we are trusting them to try again to follow through. Trust is something we keep giving over and over again.

After we have dealt with a challenging behavior, we put this experience behind us. Next time, we offer a fresh start – and the chance to do the right thing.

Can It Get Any Worse?   APRIL 20

Yes! When we are in the middle of tough times, everything seems impossible. We wonder how we will ever work this out.

> Our child is having difficulty at school.
> Loneliness surfaces when a friend moves.
> We are still recovering after a visit from
>   extended family.

Some experiences are very tough to deal with, but we can and we do. Our attitude helps us survive tough times. We can decide how to react to this situation –

> "This is horrible and impossible and I will never
> get past this."
>   Or
> "This is awful, but the kids and I will get
> through this."

Even if things get worse before they get better, we have what we need to effectively deal with this now. We can pay attention to our physical and mental health needs. We can connect with supportive people. We can adopt a "can do" positive attitude. With time, self-care, support, and patience, "this too shall pass."

Learning to Laugh   APRIL 21

Sometimes something just strikes us as hilarious. We laugh out loud, even though we may be the only one laughing. Humor is an important emotional release. When we laugh, chemicals are released in our brains that elevate our mood. Letting a big belly laugh rock us to the core just feels good! We laugh when something feels funny. We laugh when things do not go as we expected. It is also helpful to be able to laugh at ourselves, relaxing when we have made a silly mistake.

Humor is a learned response. Remember an infant's first smile? We smile at them and they respond. Eventually smiles turn into giggles that shake their whole body. For some, a sense of humor comes naturally. Others are very serious and sensitive. They need to work at it, nurturing their silliness and allowing themselves to relax and play.

It feels so good when something just cracks us up and we laugh out loud. When we laugh *with* children, we are helping each other to see the humor in many situations.

Hey, is this really so serious? Smile and experience the lighter side of life.

Expressing Needs and Wants   APRIL 22

> You gave your child 30 minutes of computer time and set a timer. After several minutes, he runs to you in a panic and screeches, "I can't do it! I need you to fix it."

Our first impulse may be to complain right back, "Stop whining!" But, take a breath.

> "I know you can fix it. What would help you right now?"
>
> "Mom, the timer's ticking. I'm going to have to reboot the computer. I won't have any time to play the game. Can I have some extra time to play?"
>
> "Sure, once you get the game going, we'll reset the timer."

Sometimes children have a hard time telling us exactly what's bothering them. As their frustration takes the lead, they forget to ask for what they really need or want. Our patient understanding and clear questions can help them figure this out and communicate more effectively. Children learn to solve their conflicts as a result of positive interactions.

Doing What's Right APRIL 23

Understanding the differences between right and wrong is one of the important lessons of childhood. Doing what's right often means demonstrating kindness to others, being honest, cooperating, and being responsible. We frequently reward this behavior with acknowledgment – "Good for you. You worked hard to get all of your homework done."

We want children to develop the courage to resist doing the wrong things. We want them to avoid going along with the group when they know it's not the right thing to do. We want them to be polite and wait instead of pushing themselves to the front of the line. We want them to remember to resist doing or saying things which are hurtful to others.

> "I know you felt a lot of pressure from your
> friends to do that. I am proud of you for stand-
> ing up for what you thought was right."

Children are encouraged to do what's right when we are good role models. They also appreciate it when we let them know we notice their strengths.

Sibling Rivalry APRIL 24

It's only natural. Brothers and sisters have been fighting and vying for their parents' attention forever! There is often a pecking order of authority. Oldest brother or sister rules the others. They believe the youngest is spoiled and gets away with things that they never could. Jealousy happens as they struggle to be on top.

But it does not have to be a competition. And we certainly don't want a war. Children have different personalities and needs. We want to let them know that they are each special in their own way! Each of them wants our attention. Though this may not feel equal, our attention should be fair and based on individual needs.

We can't avoid all of the conflicts that arise between siblings, but we can set the stage for understanding. We can teach them conflict resolution skills so they can reach fair settlements. We can encourage an atmosphere of friendship and cooperation. Children can learn valuable social skills in the challenging, yet loving environment of family life.

Sleep, My Little One, Sleep   APRIL 25

You were busy today. You went on one errand too many. Your child was very patient considering all the times you got into and out of the car for *just one more* stop. And so, at 4 p.m., he crashed, out cold, and slept for over an hour. Uh-oh! You know what this will mean. Tonight's bedtime will be way off! He won't be tired at the usual time.

After an evening with all the regular routines – bath, tooth brushing, story time – now it's time for bed. If he resists when you scoop him up to carry him to bed, show you understand, "I know it's hard to go to bed. But it is time now and I will be right here in the morning. You can come get me when you wake up." Hug him close, gently deliver him to bed, rub his back, talk about the busy day, and reassure him.

Even if he gets up again, be patient. If you keep the house very quiet, with the TV off, this too can encourage sleep because he is not as likely to feel he is missing anything.

When children fight sleep, the worse thing to do is to fight back. What can help? Soft music, back rubs, quiet activity, our calm voice, and understanding.

First Prize   APRIL 26

It is very rare to win a first prize in any kind of contest. Some of us are not even competitive enough or brave enough to enter a contest. But most of us have gotten some kind of recognition through the years for small accomplishments.

And admittedly, this feels good!

Children shine when they receive acknowledgment for their efforts.

"Good job."

"Thank you. That was helpful."

"You're number one in my book."

"You get first prize for Saturday room cleaning."

When children receive affirmation, they learn how to give back in the same spirit of appreciation.

"You're the best mom."

"You are Number One, dad!"

"Thanks for the yummy cookies."

We all appreciate it when we receive genuine recognition from someone we care about.

Peace Begins at Home APRIL 27

Creating peace is a family matter. In our daily interactions, we are always teaching children how to deal with conflict. To resolve issues that come up, we can take an authoritarian stance. "We're going to do it my way, no negotiations!" Or we can choose the more difficult, but also more rewarding path of peace.

The path to peace requires a willingness to listen and seek what is best for all concerned. The path to peace is one of respect. We work to reach a fair decision that has looked at all sides of an issue.

When children grow up in this kind of environment, they learn the tools they will need to resolve the conflicts that naturally arise in life. They will be able to negotiate with friends and school mates, and later with work mates and life partners.

Doing things *my way* separates and alienates us from each other. Peace is not the easy way. Peace *is* the only way to fairness. The way of peace brings people together.

Forgiving Ourselves

After asking your child three times to stop playing and come in to do chores, and getting no response, you lost it. You screamed and fumed. She finally came in, but the guilt monster came along, too. This is not the way you want to interact with your child.

Everyone makes mistakes. But we usually hold ourselves to very high standards. We become angry with ourselves and embarrassed. We are not proud of our reactive behavior. We are imperfect beings. And, fortunately, we can still learn.

We need to be kind to ourselves and remember that even when our interactions are less than understanding, love has usually been at the heart of our outburst. We want the best for children. We want them to grow into caring, responsible adults.

So, after our outburst, we can apologize. Most of the time, they have already forgiven us. "That's okay mom, everyone gets angry sometimes."

Now it's time for the more difficult task of forgiving ourselves and letting it go. Maybe next time we will remember to take a breath before responding.

Asking for Help

We weren't meant to do this alone. But sometimes we feel alone. We have asked ourselves, "How can one child possibly have such a huge impact on my life?" Caring for children is a very big responsibility. Sometimes it feels like all of our energy and resources are drained!

Whether you are a single parent, a stay-at-home parent whose primary role is raising children, or a teacher, you know how difficult this is to do on your own. Everything falls on your shoulders!

What we need at these times is support. But, it can be hard to ask for help. Who do you fall back on? Who is behind you, offering strong arms when you feel overwhelmed and exhausted? Who can you talk to when you're feeling frustrated and the kids are finally in bed? Where can you get some support today?

It's hard to ask for help, but we must! Call someone. Take a walk with a friend. We are energized by knowing that we are not alone. Someone is there for us.

Planting Seeds

Every day we are planting seeds. As children, we planted seeds in a little cup and set them on a window sill. We gave our seeds sun and water and nutrients. We watched them every day. Eventually, the new plant broke through the soil – when ready and on its own timeline. Before our young eyes, the plant continued to grow and reach for the light.

Children must also be planted in fertile soil. Who and what they will become is partly a reflection of our attitudes, values, and conduct.

What kind of attitudes do you want to plant and nurture to full flower? Impatience and anger? "Hurry up! Do it right now!" or "I'm too busy." Some sprouts survive even when we ignore them. Or will you plant love, patience, kindness, and time to listen?

When we plant seeds with care and provide the nutrients of love and support, children are more likely to blossom and thrive.

May

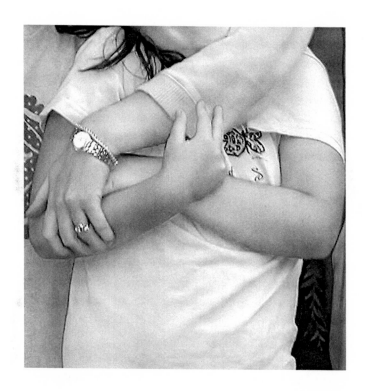

Looking into a Crystal Ball

We have all had this wish – "Wouldn't it be nice to see into the future?" But, alas, the future is forever a mystery. In spite of that, we still wonder:

> They fight so much. *Will they ever be friends?*
>
> She has a hard time in social situations. *When will she be comfortable around her peers?*
>
> He struggles with school. *Will he eventually find a job that he loves?*
>
> She is sick often. *Will she grow out of these ear infections?*

There is one thing that we can count on with children – as soon as we think we have figured out this stage in their development, something changes. And all is mystery again.

We can't predict their future, but we can do our best to provide a solid foundation today, built on trust – trusting the process that takes each child on the inevitable journey to adulthood. We can offer our love and encouragement as each child moves along a unique path.

Saying "Yes"

Adults can help keep young children safe by child-proofing the environment. We place out of reach or secure those things that are dangerous or inappropriate for children. We put away things that are attractive and create a constant "no" struggle. By child-proofing, we are creating a "yes" environment –

> Saying "yes" to safe exploration
>
> Saying "yes" to healthy choices
>
> Saying "yes" to time for play
>
> Saying "yes" to cuddle time

Creating a "yes" environment with healthy limits gives young children freedom to explore. This opens up a world of possibilities for learning. A child's self-esteem and confidence are enhanced by the opportunity to safely test his own abilities. This positive environment also lessens the negative energy of "No!" between adults and children. A "yes" environment says –

"You are capable. I trust you to explore and learn!"

Saying "No!" MAY 3

When we say "No," it is important that we mean what we say and follow through.

"No, it is not okay to play outside right now.
We are going to eat dinner in five minutes."

When children nag and plead and we give in, saying, "Whatever! Just leave me alone!" they learn that our "No" is not serious, and that nagging, whining, and pleading work to get what they want.

Instead, we can think before we respond. Sometimes when we are stressed, we quickly blurt out a "No!" and regret it in the next moment. If our first response was "No, you can't," but our second thought is "Why not?" we can say "I'm sorry, I was too quick to say 'No.' It is okay with me if you do that. Just remember to be back here by five o'clock."

We can prevent this waffling by thinking before responding. How important is this right now? Does it really matter? Could this request be okay or workable?

Sometimes "No" is necessary, but we can think before making this our automatic response. Children want to be able to count on us. They need consistent limits. We need to mean what we say and say what we mean.

Surprise! MAY 4

Your son is in a school assembly. You decide to go and you sneak into the back during the presentations. Your son has prepared a brief speech. You are bursting with pride. Then, while everyone else waits on stage listening to the next presenter, your child walks off the stage and heads to the back of the hall where he notices you are standing.

You're thinking, "What is he doing? This is so embarrassing! He's supposed to be waiting up there with everyone else. I'll have to talk to him later about this."

He makes his way back to you. In the midst of the great hall with many of his friends and their families watching, he steps up right beside you and gives you a squeeze. "Thanks for coming, Mom. Love you." With renewed appreciation for your son, "I love you, too." With that assurance, he walks back to rejoin those on the stage.

We are sometimes so quick to assume or judge children's responses. If we wait and listen, we just might be surprised by a very different reward – "Love you, Mom."

On Overload   MAY 5

> Child care before and after school
> School 8am to 3pm
> Weekly piano lessons and daily practicing
> Soccer team practice
> Periodic appointments
> Play dates with friends
> Weekend religious school
> Homework
> Evening routines

Daily life feels crazy sometimes, as we shuttle children from activity to activity. When do they have time to just *be* kids? This includes leisure time. Time to relax. Time to play in the neighborhood. Time to choose to read or play a game. Time for fun.

Daily life can become like a fast paced, non-stop merry-go-round. Along with this comes stress and illness.

Or, we can take time to enjoy our days. We can spend time together and occasionally let our schedules take care of themselves. We can remember to avoid filling our days so full of activities and appointments that we leave no time for fun. We all need time to relax and play.

Expect the Best MAY 6

Some children seem to be born with confidence. If something proves difficult, they are willing to try again and again. Others are more easily discouraged.

No matter what a child's natural temperament tendencies, labels are not helpful. Positive affirmations are.

> "I know you can do it."
>
> "I'm sure if you think about it, you'll find a better idea."
>
> "Your project is very creative."
>
> "You are playing very nicely with your little sister."

These positive statements help children believe in themselves and their own potential. If we expect the worst, we often see it. When we expect the best, children can reach new heights. They will try hard to demonstrate the expectations that we have for them. They want to do their best.

Power Sharing MAY 7

Do you ever ask yourself – who's in charge here? Just about as soon as a toddler learns to walk, the need to share our power begins. When a newborn comes into this world, who has the power? The infant must! It is our job to interpret the foreign language of the child's cries. What is needed now? Food, comfort, a dry diaper, or some stimulation? Adults respond as best they can to the infant's needs.

As children grow, communication skills increase. Toddlers understand some words long before they master the ability to express themselves. When we say, "I hear you. I'll be right with you," toddlers learn to wait.

Young children have a strong desire for independence. She wants to do it her way, "Me do it!" Then in the next moment, she falls to the ground in tears when you aren't responding quickly enough to help her. She wants the power, but doesn't know how to handle it.

As children grow and their ability to make decisions increases, they become more capable of sharing the power. As they demonstrate more self-control, we give them new choices. We want them to make safe choices and use their power wisely. We can teach children about sharing the power, working together, and making healthy choices. But, we must be willing to share, too.

Mother's Day

Every day can be Mother's Day, but on the second Sunday in May we remember mothers. We have not all had supportive relationships with our moms growing up or even in recent years. But, Mother's Day is a time to look back with a generous heart at the women who helped to shape us. Today, we remember all of the things that mothers do to help children grow.

> We remember her sacrifices, as she made
> something possible for us.
> We remember her laughter.
> We remember her tears of joy and of concern.
> We remember her pride in us when we did
> well.
> We remember her frustrations and hurt when
> we got into trouble.
> We remember our resistance to her requests,
> and her persistence with us – anyway.
> We remember the way she stuck up for us
> when someone was giving us grief.
> We remember her encouragement, cheering us
> on from the sidelines.
> We remember hot meals...or any special meal.
> We remember the love – in all its forms.
> Thanks, Mom.

Who Knows Best?

We adults don't *always* know best. When children are very little, they need protective parents and teachers who are looking out for their best interests. Even though we can't fully imagine their future, we can offer them varied experiences and encourage learning that will equip them to face whatever awaits them.

Adults don't always know what's best, but we *do* our best to help them by making healthy choices for them, finding appropriate schooling, encouraging positive friendships, and providing opportunities for learning.

By about 11 or 12 years old, children are already making many of their own choices, based on their interests, talents, social needs, abilities, and temperament. By mid-adolescence, adults are reminded daily that *our* lesson is about trust. Teens already have many of the life skills they will need.

Offering choices encourages children to think about what they want or need right now and what is best for them. We are saying, "I trust you. I know you can figure out what you need. You are capable. You know what is best for you."

Double Standards

What behaviors or activities are truly acceptable for adults, but not for kids? Even though there are some things that adults can do which are not appropriate for children, generally, there are very few behaviors that require a true *double standard*. Adults go to bed later than children. Adults sometimes have foods which children may not appreciate. Adults monitor the use of medications when needed. Adults watch some television and movies which are not appropriate for children.

When children ask, "Why can't I do that?" we can find ways to honestly communicate the differences. "I know you are curious about this book, but this is an adult book. Let's go read one of your favorites."

We want children to respect themselves and others. Most

of the behaviors that are not okay for them are not healthy or respectful for us either. What is good for children is often good for us.

Chore Wars

"You need to stop what you are doing right now and come in here to clean up all of these toys."

"What's so great about clean and neat?"

"Hey, I'm not the maid!"

"You're not my boss. You can't make me!"

"Oh yes I can. We're turning the TV off until you clean up!"

Frowning, with arms crossed tightly on the chest and feet planted, the lines are drawn. The battle is on. We know this conflict well.

No one likes being ordered around while the commander stands at attention and barks orders. Children are more likely to cooperate when we do it together.

When will they be able to do their chores without help or a reminder? Well, some are born organized and want things tidy, but this is rare. Children need reminders. We can give a warning:

"In ten minutes we're all going to work on this room, straighten things up, and get some laundry going."

A gentle reminder and a genuine spirit of cooperation can prevent the chore wars.

Good Grief

How can the loss of anyone or anything that has been special be a good thing? When someone we love dies or moves away, there is often a gaping hole. We each grieve at our own pace. In time, we can work our way through the hurt.

When children grieve, they don't always know how to

talk about what they are feeling, and neither do we. They may feel angry. They may irrationally believe that they did something to make this happen. When children are sad, their whole body tells us. Their behavior may be wild. Their eating and sleeping routines can be totally off. Just like adults, they need support and understanding to get through this tough time.

When we are the one who is sad, children want to help us feel better. So, we need to reach out and let others know what they can do to provide help. During hard times, we really need each other. Together, we can come to accept this loss in our lives.

Negative Attention MAY 13

Children want our attention, whatever they can get from us. Positive attention occurs when we acknowledge their behaviors in encouraging ways. This kind of reaction is usually satisfying for both of us.

When we are distracted or involved in another activity, we can count on children to act in ways that demand our attention. Now! Sometimes we respond with a negative reaction. We snap off our own verbal demand, "What!?!" Or, we restrict or ground or punish.

Though it may seem like he is trying to get a rise out of us, we can learn to control our reaction. We can stop and think first. Then, we can respond patiently with well thought out words.

Sometimes children need to be guided to a more appropriate behavior. When we think before we react, we are more likely to give them the positive attention they need right now.

Standing Firm with Love MAY 14

Adolescents rebel. They fight for their independence, and at the same time, they want us to do things for them, right now! They promise to do their homework and chores and conveniently claim they forgot when we notice it isn't done.

They have excuses. "I didn't say I would do that."

What is our responsibility? When can we let go and let them experience their own consequences? Adolescents need us more than they realize and certainly more than they will admit. They need us to stand firm with appropriate limits, because we care.

Our response has a greater chance of success when we remain calm, yet firm. "I know you want to go out with your friends. I want to remind you that you have some other responsibilities to complete first. When they are done, you can do what you choose."

These hassles and frustrating interactions are not fun. But, they are necessary. Teens need limits, too. We can respond from the heart.

Home Run!   MAY 15

Sometimes it feels like we are "on a roll." Everything is falling into place. Though people are more likely to need support when times are tough, we all appreciate a cheering section behind us that recognizes our successes! "Good one!" or "All right, you did it!"

Children like these affirmations, too. Though many parents and teachers are generous with this praise, we are still more likely to make a comment when there has been a mistake. In the long run, it is the positive encouragement which motivates. Positive feedback helps us feel willing to stand up and try again.

Everyone benefits from genuine encouragement and recognition. We can offer encouragement in good times *and* when there are struggles.

Perfectland   MAY 16

Is it really so perfect in Perfectland? There is not a hair out of place. Clothes are all clean and match beautifully. Children always obey and do what they are told. But, do these people know how to have fun? Can kids be kids in Perfectland?

What is really important, anyway? We want children to know we love them. We can encourage their creativity. We demonstrate our flexibility and understanding when we show our appreciation for them, just as they are!

When we have unrealistic expectations for children, sometimes they feel like they can't do anything right. They never can do enough to reach the impossible expectation of eventual perfection.

We all make mistakes. We all have flaws. Children are not perfect. Neither are we. But, we each have a lot to offer, just as we are!

Reaching Out   MAY 17

A dad remembers an experience which helped to strengthen his commitment toward his son. When his son was first born, it all felt very foreign. As a very young man, he was in a fog for months and felt awkward even holding the baby. Then, while hanging out in the living room one day, he watched his infant son as he was crawling under and around the glass coffee table. The baby had been working on standing and moving around the furniture. At one point a tiny hand reached out and dad reached back, offering a finger. That tight, tiny grip said it all: "You're my dad. I need you in my life to offer guidance and support."

That moment was a turning point that this dad can clearly visualize years later. He has been there, communicating regularly with his son's teachers. He has only missed one of his games in all of these years. He has encouraged him with school work and home chores. No one in his life is more important to him than his son, and it shows!

Doing the Baby Dance   MAY 18

Your friend is holding his infant daughter, gently swaying side to side as he rocks her to sleep – the Baby Dance. As her eyes get heavy and she nods off, you realize you have been swaying, too. Why do adults enjoy holding someone close, dancing to the music in the background? Could it be that we relax almost reflexively as we remember the soothing comfort of long ago?

Before birth, infants experience a rhythmic dance at all times – steady heartbeat and the rocking movement of mother's body as she goes about her day. Expectant mothers often notice the baby's movement most when they are still and quiet themselves. Maybe this is the beginning of self-soothing. Some infants learn to rock themselves back and forth when they are trying to put themselves to sleep.

Older children sometimes like listening to music or snuggling close as someone quietly reads to them. This close contact does not spoil babies. Older children still need it, too. So do we. There is comfort in this gentle connection. Dance on.

Emergency Preparedness MAY 19

No matter what we might do to prevent illness and injury, some things just happen. They are out of our control, be it a devastating storm or a bad case of the flu. But, we can prepare children so that instead of feeling fearful, they feel more of a sense of control.

What's most important in an emergency? The people! There are steps we can take to do our best to keep everyone safe. A check list helps us remember what precious things to take with us when we have only minutes to react, including people, papers, pictures.

Create an emergency plan and talk about this together so that everyone knows where to go and how to stay in touch. Know where the most important items are located so you can find them quickly.

Preparedness can help prevent panic. If an unexpected crisis does come up, children need reassurance that we are looking out for them and doing everything we can to keep them safe.

Time To Go Home

Why is it that the same child who resists being dropped off at child care or school in the morning can create a horrible fuss at pick-up time? The teacher says, "She had a great day." And the parent thinks, "Why is this happening? I'm tired. I missed my child and looked forward to our reunion. But right now I feel unappreciated."

This reaction on the part of the child can be understood in several ways. The child may be having a good time. It is not easy for anyone to stop when they are having fun. A fight may happen if we insist on an immediate departure. So, it helps if we can enter quietly and give a five minute warning, letting the child finish and clean up.

Some children hold themselves together during the day. Then, once the parent arrives, they feel freer to discharge their pent-up energy from all the day's frustrations. A parent's quiet voice and relaxed body language can help reassure the child.

At the end of a busy day, patient adults offer soothing support that sets the stage for a more relaxed evening.

Cooking Together

Preparing meals is one of the daily activities that must be done, just like laundry, cleaning up, and shopping. Children are much more likely to participate when we include them from a very early age. Then they learn that this is something families *share!*

Even though we may worry that including children in meal preparation will take longer, and will most certainly be messier, it can also be fun. In fact, the benefits of working together usually far outweigh the hassles.

When children help us, they are learning how to take care of themselves. We are reinforcing social skills as we interact. Children can develop patience as they wait for it to be all done. Cooking reinforces math skills. Children are also more likely to eat what they've helped prepare.

Family time is about enjoying each other, even when we are doing our chores.

Figuring It Out   MAY 22

Learning is a gradual process. When a baby is born, she is not aware of the important tool at the end of her arm – the hand. Then at about two months old, she notices her hands and stares at her fingers. She tentatively reaches toward a curiosity and bats at it. Soon she can pinch together her fingers to pick up something. Finally, the ability to grasp anything is conquered. From now on, everything is fair game, and often goes directly into her mouth. She is learning that hands are valuable tools.

Similarly, an infant does not realize that a car is a valuable tool. Awareness grows as the toddler sits at the steering wheel and makes car noises with excitement. The school-aged child knows that someday a car will get him where he wants to go. But not until the teen years does he actually get a chance to learn how to drive. Feet and hands struggle at first to coordinate the whole process. Finally, he's got it, and passes the driving test.

Sometimes learning seems to happen overnight, but it is actually a slow and steady process. At all points along the way, our support can encourage exploration and learning.

Cinderella   MAY 23

This childhood favorite is a story about stepfamilies and unconditional love. "Mom always loved you best." This really isn't supposed to be a competition. Every child deserves love and attention. Each child has unique needs.

"Step" in this context implies *a step away from.* But, stepparents are real parents, no matter how they got there. All parents share the important role of raising healthy, loved children. Being a stepparent can definitely be hard. Children never fully let go of the special places in their hearts for their parents.

The storybook Cinderella succeeded in life, in spite of her non-supportive stepmother and stepsisters. Many stepfamilies reflect a far more positive image of family life. Stepparents can offer acceptance and love. They can be approachable and make themselves available for conversation and support.

Out in Public   MAY 24

Children seem to have antennae which tell them how we are feeling. Sometimes it seems like they know when we are feeling vulnerable. We are embarrassed when their behavior is inappropriate in public. Maybe someone is watching. Children realize that we are less likely to reinforce necessary limits. They have learned that there is more latitude when other people are around.

But, children really need the same adult response in public settings that they experience at home or at school. If we are embarrassed, we are allowing their behavior to reflect on us. But, does it really? Even if she lies on the floor and lets loose with a huge tantrum, this need not reflect on you. She's tired. She wants something that she can't have. Maybe this behavior is just saying she is bored or would rather be doing something else right now.

In these moments, we need to remember to think about how she is feeling. Talk with her quietly, and if needed, leave with as little of a scene as possible. We can maintain our sensitivity to children's needs, even in public.

Time Out to Relax   MAY 25

Children are running around, screaming. Their energy is overwhelming. It seems like every other minute they are fighting. Your nerves are frazzled. It's been a long, hectic day. Your patience is worn thin.

Stop! Take a break. Change the energy.

Breathe!

You can ask the kids to join you in a time-out to quiet

down and relax. They can get back to their game or activity in a few minutes, but a break will do you all good. This is not a punishment. This is meant to be an energizer. If this is a common routine, they will participate without much resistance, because they have learned that it feels good.

Set a timer for ten minutes of quiet. Put on soft music. Get a cool washcloth for your forehead or the back of your neck. Sit down and put your feet up.

Breathe!

"I'm Sorry" MAY 26

If we want children to learn to admit their mistakes, to accept responsibility, and even to apologize, it starts with us. Adults make mistakes, too. We speak harshly. We say "no" too quickly and sometimes regret it. We say we will do something, then we don't. We miss opportunities to listen to or play together.

Apologizing is not a sign of weakness. It is a strength. When we say "I'm sorry," we show children part of a whole person who is sad sometimes, has fun sometimes, gets tired sometimes, learns new things sometimes, and who makes mistakes – sometimes.

There is a well-known phrase from a movie some years back, "Love means never having to say you're sorry." Absolutely not! Loving someone means we care enough to admit our mistakes, and say "I'm sorry," genuinely. "I'm sorry I yelled." "I'm sorry I wasn't paying attention." "I'm sorry we didn't have time to do that today." Our sincere apology means we love each other no matter what.

"Say You're Sorry" MAY 27

Your child has just been rude to you and snapped when you made a request. Or, she is frustrated by an interaction and just hit or grabbed a toy. Or, your son said something that hurt someone's feelings. Even though these behaviors can be disappointing or embarrassing to us, each child has some responsibility for these interactions. It almost always takes two.

In the heat of the moment, if we ask children to, "Say you're sorry!" they may not be. We have all heard children obey and say "Sor-ry" with a sneer and a whine. This does not feel sincere because it probably isn't.

It is not a good idea to *require* an apology. Before play resumes, we can ask children, "Is there anything you need to say or do before you go back to playing again?" Usually children will have something to suggest, like, "Hey, let's do something else that we *both* want to play." One or both of them may even apologize on their own.

Eventually, we want children to learn to acknowledge their regrets sincerely. We all make mistakes!

A Few Moments of Peace   MAY 28

The commitment to take time for ourselves seems so hard to do with all the demands of a busy day and equally busy children. But it is possible. We deserve this important self- care.

Giving ourselves a few minutes can restore our energy and patience. We can choose what works for us –

> Brew some tea and put your feet up;
> Listen to your favorite music;
> Sit on the floor and do some gentle stretches;
> Cuddle with your child;
> Read a book;
> Sit quietly in thought and breathe.

Let the next task that is calling you wait. Your work will still be there in 15 minutes. And a little rest can go a long way toward renewing your spirits! We really can make time for a few minutes of peace. Children need patient adults who are revived by this self-care.

Parents' Night Out

Adults deserve a break from the demands of 24-7 non-stop parenting. But, it can be hard to find someone to care for our child. "No one can care for my child like I would. I can't trust anyone." Maybe so, but we can not be at our best unless we take care of ourselves. We need to recharge our batteries to have the energy to meet our daily challenges.

Taking time for ourselves doesn't have to cost money. Sometimes we are rejuvenated by an evening walk. A drive with our favorite music playing can be relaxing. Dinner out with a picnic or visiting a restaurant is a treat. A movie can be a welcome diversion. We can also attend a parenting group or other class to gain more confidence.

Self-care is not selfish! It is important to reach out to others and ask for help. We can find a family member, a friend, or a sitter whom we can trust.

Right Before My Eyes

All during a child's development we notice steps toward maturity. But adolescence can still feel unexpected and especially overwhelming! Imagine how frustrating and scary it must feel for them to deal with the physical changes. Their body feels foreign to them. Some changes are subtle while others seem to happen overnight. To us, it feels like we are living with a child inside an adult body.

Beyond the physical changes, there are many social and emotional adjustments that are made well into their twenties. Along the way, we can support them. Sometimes they want our help, while also seeking independence. We can encourage healthy choices. We can keep the doors of communication open. We can offer them opportunities to participate in the adult world through work and inclusion in inter-generational activities.

If your child is not here yet, you have time. If your child has reached adolescence, you can continue to maintain a supportive relationship. Children grow so quickly.

Two youngsters were darting up and down the tree trunk, shiny fur, fluffy tails. Mama squirrel came up the trunk and scurried onto a branch, then jumped onto the rooftop. The little ones seemed comfortable going higher into the tree and moved ably among the branches, but they would *not* take the leap to the roof. They went back down the trunk and played in safer territory. Mama watched from the roof then back tracked down the trunk. Up she came again with youngsters following close behind. Let's try this again. Up and down, again and again. She was certainly a model of patience and persistence. Well, the little ones would have nothing to do with that leap, so they all went somewhere else to try other squirrely acrobatics.

Of course, there are countless human examples of parental patience. But we often forget that learning is on the child's timeline, not our own. We sometimes push children to be potty-trained, to read early, to sit still at the dinner table, to act properly, to dress like a grown-up. But at what cost? It is so much better to follow each child's lead for learning when their interest and readiness are present.

June

June Is Busting Out All Over JUNE 1

Summer is right around the corner. School is nearly over for another year. Parents and teachers can feel the trapped energy. There may be vacations and special activities planned. But, most of all, children are looking forward to a break from school routines.

We can help children ease into this transition with realistic expectations. It is difficult for children to concentrate on class work at the end of the school year. It helps to complete projects in small steps, asking them to focus their attention in short spurts. We can give them breaks between activities. Busy kids need opportunities to play hard *and* to rest.

We can begin to plan for summer. What do I need to schedule so that my child has fun and learns, too? What activities help my child stay fit – physically, emotionally, socially and academically? How can I also find a little time for *me* this summer?

June brings the promise of summer ahead. Enjoy!

Relationships Take Care JUNE 2

Relationships don't just happen. They need attention and nutrients, just like our gardens. If we want children to feel connected to us, we must spend time creating this close tie.

Relationships grow within the fertile soil of love and communication. Children feel close to us when we pay attention to them. We can also acknowledge their feelings and answer their questions.

Relationships are nurtured by the gift of time. Children like it when we follow their lead into play. They like it when we plan activities that everyone can enjoy or even when we just hang out together.

Relationships are also fostered by connection – hugs, a gentle hand on the shoulder, a smile. These add warmth, as long as we respect a child's wishes and back off when the child asks for a little space.

Every day we can nurture our relationships.

Celebrate Rites of Passage

We live in a culture that often forgets the important celebrations associated with rites of passage. We slip through life without recognizing the accomplishments that are part of our growth from one milestone to the next.

There are many events which could easily qualify as significant passages –

first tooth	first shave
sleeping all night	going to high school
first steps	first date
first words	driver's license
first day of school	first real job
learning to read	graduation
first sleep over	moving out
a new school year	going off to college
signs of puberty	getting married
first period	birth of a baby

We can mark these "firsts" and celebrate. Quietly light a candle. Share this moment with others. Make a toast to this special time – We made it! She did it! He finally got there!

The Tooth Fairy

Losing that first tooth is a day to remember. Though there are still many years and more wiggly teeth ahead, permanent adult teeth are pushing their way into position. This is not an easy time for some children who are nervous when the tooth moves. They won't touch it and patiently wait for it to come out on its own. Other children can't keep their hands out of their mouth. They are eager to get that tooth out and under their pillow. Children need to move at their own pace and in their own way.

Losing a tooth can also be a symbolic time. No longer a baby, at five or six years old, children are moving into the "age of reason." The first five years of life have set a foundation for all future learning experiences. By the time children lose their first tooth, they have learned much of the basic knowledge they will need to function in the world – communication, emotional sensitivity, caring, basic self-care, problem solving. Future learning will refine these skills.

So, maybe the tooth fairy is a guardian for this important *rite of passage*. When she leaves a coin or a prize, she is saying, "You're growing up. This is an exciting time!"

Promises to Keep JUNE 5

Keeping a promise says: "You can trust me." and "I believe in you." It hurts a child when we say we'll do something and we don't. Sometimes unexpected events occur and we have to change our plans. If this happens rarely, children quickly forgive and forget.

But, if we break our promises often, children lose faith in us. They learn that we do not honor our commitments. In order to keep our trust intact, we must learn to think before we commit. We must be very careful to make promises only when we are sure we can follow through.

> "I would really like to do that, but I am not sure if we will have the time. If we can't fit it in today, let's talk about how we can plan for that another time."

"I promise to love you forever." "I promise to be here for you, no matter what!" We can make promises that we know we will be able to honor, no matter what comes up.

"Because!" JUNE 6

You have just asked him to stop playing and put his toys away. His response, "Why do I have to?" Yours? "Because I said so!"

First, children deserve our respect in all of our encounters. This kind of reply has a sharp, disrespectful edge. "Because" is not a helpful response. Children do not need a long explanation. But, they do deserve a simple answer which will help them understand. Some examples are:

> "That's dangerous!"
>
> "This is not a good time for that."
>
> "That's not your toy. Let's go find one of yours."
>
> "I'm really tired right now."
>
> "Now it's time for lunch. We can do that a little later."

Saying "Because" alone just does not give enough information. Children are much more likely to follow through when we offer a respectful and reasonable explanation.

"I Hate You!" JUNE 7

What adult does not cringe at the sound of these hurtful words coming from a beloved child? How we respond to these words impacts how often we will hear them.

Don't take it personally! This child does not hate you. Yes, she is feeling angry or frustrated right now. Maybe you have put a limit on some behavior. Or, he may be unhappy with your authority and wants to feel more personal control over choices and decisions.

These words are often thrown as a weapon with the hope that they will influence us. We can let our healthy response be a healthy lesson.

First, acknowledge feelings –

> "I know you're disappointed, but we can't do what you want right now."

Reaffirm your commitment –

> "I love you even when you are angry at me."

Give a cooling off period before resolving this –

> "I know you are angry right now. When you are ready we can try again."

When children realize that our love is unconditional, they feel safe enough to let all feelings out, even hateful anger.

"You're Not Listening!"

Many parents have said, "My child just won't listen to me!" Actually, children usually hear us. But, they may be so involved in an activity that they don't want to be interrupted. Or they may have learned to tune us out.

We don't always pay attention either. We interrupt children when we don't realize what is going on. We can change our behavior by noticing what he is doing. Then, get down on his level, get eye contact, and gently make your request.

When children say, "You're not listening to me," it is often true. Sometimes we get so involved in our own activities or expectations that we are not willing to stop and listen and really hear what they are saying.

Instead, we *can* stop and give our undivided attention with strong eye contact. One of the most important gifts we will ever give children is to be approachable and really listen.

Big Brother/Big Sister

It is not always fun to be the big brother or big sister. It can be difficult and demanding. We constantly remind them that they are a role model for their younger siblings. We want them to take care of their siblings and protect them from harm. We want them all to love and respect each other. We may even expect older children to be responsible, well beyond their years.

There are also rewards that come with being the oldest. There are privileges that this child receives that younger siblings have not yet earned – staying up later, watching certain TV shows, being included in some adult conversations. But, certainly, there are times when big brothers and big sisters say that the privileges just aren't worth it.

It is our job to balance the willingness of a child to be helpful and in charge of a situation, with the very real need to just be a kid and not have to take care of someone else.

"Yes, you are the big sister. And it is my job to look after you both."

Confessions of an Imperfect Parent

Even though we know better, we sometimes lose our patience. We get frustrated when children say, "Yeah, I know," to our third request and continue to sit there and play. We know what we *should* say or do, but in the moment, we forget. Certain things just trigger a harsh reaction in us. When we're stressed, we forget to stop before reacting, and check in with ourselves –

> *What is going on for me right now?*
> *How am I feeling? Overwhelmed? Hurried?*
> *Pleased?*

Sometimes children deliver valuable wisdom. "Calm down, Mom. I'll be right there." And he's right. He needs time to get to a place to pause his activity, and we need to take a breath, relax, and take care of our self. Is this really such a big deal?

After doing what was requested, he delivers more adolescent wisdom with a comforting teenaged hug, "Mom, relax, no one's perfect. Everyone loses it sometimes." Maybe that's what was needed in the first place – loving words and a hug.

Today Is What We Have

Too often we get caught up in our plans for tomorrow and forget to notice what is happening right in front of us, today.

Children, on the other hand, live very much in the present moment. They focus all of their energy and attention on what they are doing, right now. If we were to learn from their example, what might this mean for us?

> We would bring our curiosity into each moment.
> We would find time to play.
> We would pay attention to the details of their story.
> We would respond to questions.
> We would watch children think through an issue.

We would cherish the many tender moments that
we have together.

We would really listen, and really see, and really be – *with*
children. Rather than let it slip away, we would realize that
– Right now is the only time that really matters.

A Few More Minutes JUNE 12

In the big scheme of things, what difference does a few
more minutes make? A few minutes can make a big difference if we are talking about safety and injury prevention. But
in most situations, this won't change things much.

So give them some time to consider the next steps –

> "Okay, in a few minutes we're going to clean
> up. After you get ready for bed, we'll have time
> to read together."

Most of the fights that arise during transition times can
be prevented by giving a warning. This allows time to finish
up and prepare for the next activity.

We can lighten up. We can give a little more time to ease
the transition. We can choose our battles, and relax.

Graduation Day JUNE 13

Graduations are days to remember! It's time to kick up
our heels!! Whether graduating from preschool, elementary
school, middle school, high school, or college, this day marks
the sum total of the efforts that have been invested up to this
point. You and your child have given your energies, with
both enthusiasm and frustrations.

Your child has learned many things, gained social skills,
reached new understandings, and grown physically and emotionally. Along the way, your child has experienced struggles
and successes. All of these things have made today possible.

As we acknowledge the accomplishments, we also mark a
new beginning, right around the corner. The future is ahead.
We are proud and eager for the next steps as our child moves

on to greater independence.

Today is a day to celebrate this accomplishment. Your child has earned some special attention. Beat the drums and shout for joy. Mark this rite of passage. Wow!

Out of Balance   JUNE 14

We all feel off balance sometimes. Our emotions are skewed when we feel grumpy, frustrated, or sad. Our bodies feel off kilter when we get sick or lack energy. Our minds sometimes lose their edge and we have a hard time concentrating or forget too easily.

To keep our balance, we all need regular self-care. Some things can help us develop healthy habits.

Willingness is the first step. We must be willing to focus time and energy on our own care. Our good health also enables us to support and care for others.

Practice moderation. We get into trouble when we go to extremes. Eat enough of the right foods. Drink enough water. Do enough exercise, regularly. We really do have time for enough and can resist too much.

Be open. We get out of balance when we resist looking for new possibilities. When we see things differently, we realize that change is what we need.

Attitude is everything. We can laugh more. We can appreciate what we have. We can criticize less and let others know how special they are to us.

We can take steps today to create a healthy mental and physical sense of harmony.

Learning to Fall Better   JUNE 15

Beginner ski lessons teach how to properly get up from the inevitable fall. Beginner kayakers learn to right their boat after a tip. We all fall. The important thing is to learn to get back up and maybe even to try again.

Babies who are learning how to walk fall down and usually get right back up. They also learn very quickly to read the expressions on the faces around them. If the baby hears "oh-oh" and sees a smile, he smiles back in response, gets back up, and moves on. If the child hears a gasp and sees panic, worry, or fear, the child's reaction may be a mirror of those significant faces.

We hope children will develop the coping skills and the courage to avoid overwhelming defeat by moving on. We want them to be able to deal with a minor setback calmly.

Children model their own responses after what they have seen and heard from us. We can let them know that it is okay to fall, and then encourage them to try again.

Father's Day   JUNE 16

Father's Day is an opportunity to express our gratitude to the men in our lives who provided for us when we were growing up. We can also thank the men we know now who are important in the lives of children. Boys *and* girls both need positive male role models.

We thank fathers and father figures for their commitment to caring and their dedication to providing physical and emotional support. We thank them for –

> Being strong arms that give hugs
> Tossing the ball back and forth
> Attending school events
> Building the set for the school play
> Reading all four books at bedtime
> Getting down on the floor to play
> Applying band-aids to a "boo-boo"
> Cheering from the sidelines at a sports event
> Getting up to watch a midnight meteor shower

Father's Day is a special day of remembrance and appreciation. We don't have to wait for this special day. Thank someone today.

Amazing

Marvelous, astonishing, spectacular, incredible, wonderful – As each day, month and year passes, many incredible things happen as children develop right before our eyes. If we are watchful, we will notice:

> The observant insight of a child watching a shop door open and shut, hearing the door bell ring, and then "I get it!" realizing a sensor is setting off the bell.

> The tender comfort that a big brother shows to a frustrated little brother, after months of hassles.

> A baby's first tentative steps, soon followed by the ability to reach everything!

> The cunning way a child can very smoothly play one parent against the other to try to get what she wants.

> Hugs from teenagers.

> Comments from other adults, "Your son is such a pleasure to be around." (After you just had a big fight.)

Amazing things are happening right before our eyes.

Sleep-Overs

The first sleep-over can be another rite of passage in a child's development. Some children are more than ready for this adventure. They have been visiting grandma or trading houses with mom and dad or even with family friends since they were quite young. For others, this experience is strange and unfamiliar.

We can figure out a child's *readiness* by asking some questions –

> *How is she feeling about this? Is she expressing willingness to do this?*

*Has he demonstrated comfort with previous
separations?*

Is she comfortable with the other family?

Once children feel comfortable with the idea, some knowledge can be helpful. Remind them where you will be and how you can be reached. Make sure they know it is okay to call you at *any* time. It may also ease our minds to know the family where they will be visiting. We, too, are reassured by building in some *just in case* contingencies.

Some simple preparations can help both the eager child and the cautious child enjoy this independent time away from family.

"I Think I Can" JUNE 19

The classic children's story of *The Little Engine that Could* offers one of the early lessons about determination and persistence. We want children to develop confidence. We want them to be willing to try something new or a little difficult. We want them to be helpful. We want them to succeed.

The little engine chugged and chugged, carrying important cargo up the steep hill and down again to the waiting children. He met with adversity and challenges along the way, but he kept going. We hope children will stick with it, too, even when they run into hard times.

What is the voice saying inside the child's head? "I can't do this? I'm so stupid. I never get anything right." OR "I am determined to keep trying. It is hard, but I will get through this." Our encouragement along the way, and faith in their abilities says, "I know you can do this."

I think I can – I know I can – I did it!

Roots AND Wings JUNE 20

Some wise sages of the past have said that the two most important gifts we can offer children are roots and wings. *Roots* help to create a stable foundation with strong values like respect, honesty, appreciation and love of self and family, a sense of safety and security, and open communication. *Roots* reach deep to support growth when planted in the fertile soil of caring and understanding.

The gift of *Wings* encourages a child to fly with independence, reaching possibilities we can hardly imagine. Once children have their *Wings*, they are no longer within our control. Their choices are their own. What they become is really up to them, but our early attention to their needs helps. We can ask ourselves:

> What am I doing to provide sturdy *Roots*?
> How can I step back and help this child's
> *Wings* sprout and strengthen?

Changing Plans

JUNE 21

You had made plans to take the kids to the park and then go out to eat. But, when they woke up, you could tell right away it wasn't going to work. You thought it would be fun, but now it's not the right time.

Children are not always ready to do what we want. We can't always do what we have planned. Our good intentions do not always lead to a happy ending.

So, we need to be creative and try to figure out other activities that *will* work out. We need to shift gears and model flexibility. Timing is everything. We do not have control of every situation. Sometimes flexibility is just what is needed to get through the day successfully, even with a change of plans.

"It's Not Fair!"

JUNE 22

School-aged children say this all the time – "It's not fair!" Somewhere along the way, they get the idea that everything has to be equal or exactly the same in order to be fair. One thing we can teach them is that life is not always going to be equal. But we can reassure them that we will strive to do what's right and that's what is most fair.

Older children are allowed to stay up later. Younger children have fewer responsibilities like homework or chores. Children have different abilities and needs. "Your brother grew out of his shoes and needs a new pair. And you have grown and need a new sweatshirt. We'll deal with what you each need."

We want children to realize that we love and care for each of them, even when we don't treat them exactly the same. Our response is based on who each child is, what each child needs, and what we can do, right now. "Fair" is about paying attention to each child's special, unique needs.

Enough *JUNE 23*

It is devastating to feel like you can never have enough or do enough or be enough. This feels especially bad when someone we care about delivers this message.

"Well, you got B's and C's. Where are the A's?"

Or

"You put away your clean clothes. But, you forgot to put these dirty dishes away."

This "not enough" message says our love is only earned with acceptable behavior.

Very young children often live in the world of "enough." Not needing special tools or toys, anything becomes a toy as they play and explore with joy. They smile easily. And when they have had *enough* stimulation, they let us know!

All too quickly, children come to expect more – more things, more activities, or more attention. They can also begin to doubt themselves and feel not good enough.

Enough is about really believing that what you have and what you do and who you are is sufficient. Enough is about conveying the idea that we each have the resources of knowledge, creativity, and experience to guide us on our developmental path.

Home Alone

A child reaches another rite of passage when parents thoughtfully assess a child's readiness for the responsibility of being home alone. Children often look forward to this important step in their development.

There is no absolute right age for all children. But, there is a wrong age – when a child is not ready. Developmentally, children are rarely truly prepared to make important quick decisions before adolescence, and some not even then. When a child is too young and not prepared, calamity can occur. More important than age is maturity and an understanding of the responsibility that is being given.

Before consenting to leaving children home alone, adults need to assess a child's readiness.

> *Does she feel confident and ready for this?*
> *Does he consistently follow directions?*
> *Does she understand important safety rules?*
> *Am I comfortable with this?*

Our job is to give children a chance to practice with small steps. Then, we can celebrate together when they are ready to move forward with this new level of responsibility.

Fun on a Dime

We don't have to spend a lot of money to entertain children. In fact, it is probably better for them if they don't become accustomed to expecting expensive gifts and outings.

Children are much *less* likely to say "I'm bored" if they have learned to make their own fun. Fun can be found everywhere. And fun is often even more enjoyable when we do it *together*!

> Walk to the park.
> Take a bike ride.
> Play board or computer games.
> Read a book.
> Sing and dance.

Take a hike.
Rake the leaves and then jump in them.
Explore a creek, lake, or beach.
Make greeting cards for family and friends.
Bake some cookies or make dinner.
Play with pets.
Go swimming.

Holding a Grudge *JUNE 26*

Young children usually forgive easily. They can be very upset with a friend one minute and play happily together the next. Children rarely waste valuable time staying angry and holding a grudge. We do!

Children have a lot to teach us about how to deal with our feelings. We, too, can learn to *let it go*. When possible, we need to sit down and talk it through. Sometimes we even discover that there was a totally unintended misunderstanding.

Don't take it personally. One of us may have had a bad day and overreacted. When we hold on to our sad or angry feelings, we are the one who is hurt by unresolved issues.

We can learn together to put difficult experiences from the past behind us. We can participate in healthy conflict resolution by letting go of anger, resentment, and hurt, and moving on to better things. Relationships deserve our best.

Using Your Will-Power *JUNE 27*

In response to a child who understands school subjects, but is having a difficult time completing the work:

> "Nobody doubts that you can do this work. You are a very capable person. You're good at math. The question is not if you *can* do it, but, whether you *will* do it? Will you show your teachers what you know? Will you demonstrate that you deserve a good grade? By avoiding your homework, you are showing your WON'T-power.

Your will is up to you. That's what will-power is about, mustering the energy and resolve to do it even if it's hard or boring or seems pointless to you. It is about saying you WILL do it, even when you don't really want to."

It is a child's job to *resist*, and our job to *insist*. We gather *our* energy and stand by with support, in the midst of resistance. We can demonstrate our own loving Will-Power as we patiently work with them to reinforce theirs.

Out with the Old

JUNE 28

Much easier said than done! We become attached to the way things are...even the way things were. We are creatures of habit. So, when the time comes to put aside our old ways, it can be tough!

Children are sometimes ready to move on before we realize it. When we take the time to notice, we can see that they have learned new skills. They are ready to take on more responsibilities. They are demonstrating increased knowledge and abilities.

Our role is to trust their new abilities and encourage them.

"I know this is new for you, but I am sure you can do it. Let me know if you need some help."

As children grow, their dependence on certain toys or activities gradually slips away. We need to follow their lead. We can offer support and encouragement for their continued growth.

Attitude Adjustment

JUNE 29

Attitude takes many shapes. The words may be said or just implied with body language and tone of voice –

"I can't!"

"I don't care."

"My way is best!"

"I have more important things to do."

No matter what the attitude, the damage is done. Our relationships are hurt by this negativity and lack of cooperation.

Children's attitudes can actually be a reflection of something they heard or felt from us. Sometimes we need attitude adjustments. We can recognize the feelings in a situation and set limits without judgment.

> "I know your little brother's behavior can annoy
> you sometimes, but he loves to be with you. It is
> not okay to be rude to him."

We can also shake off our own bad attitude and communicate with sensitivity and understanding.

Stepping Back with Faith   JUNE 30

You are worried about your child. He has procrastinated and let things fall behind. Now he is very angry at himself and sounds like he may also be depressed. Protective Super Mom wants to fly in and save the day. Or you may worry that there was more that could have been taught along the way so that he would not be in trouble now. You might also feel angry about the unwise choices he made that got him here.

Even though our feelings are understandable, it is not helpful to give a lecture on sticking to a schedule. Though we may want to, hovering gives the impression that you don't believe he can do anything without you. Children need to learn to plan their own schedules and make independent decisions.

Over the years, we have loved them. We have given them opportunities for learning. We have encouraged responsibility. We have fostered their independence. Now, it's time to trust that everything will work out. He has what he needs, right now, to recover from this setback. She has everything she needs, right now, to find her own solutions. Sometimes we need to step back and have a little faith.

July

Making Progress JULY 1

Sometimes it doesn't feel like we are making any progress at all. Maybe it's time to look deeper. When we are working on doing things differently, there are almost always small changes to be made. It just takes a little longer to see bigger results. We need to be careful not to sabotage the successes by expecting miraculous improvements.

So, what are some of the little shifts you are seeing lately? With new routines, children now know more clearly what to expect. Bedtimes are going more smoothly. The children are cooperating more often. We can create back-up plans for when things don't go as expected. Some rewards and consequences are working. The children are smiling more and whining less. We are all more rested and less stressed.

Twelve-step programs of recovery stress the importance of "progress not perfection." We are making progress. We can do this, one little step at a time.

Healing the Past JULY 2

Family – these are the people who are supposed to meet our needs when we are young and love us, no matter what. They care for us when we're sick and offer help when we need a hand. Not everyone has grown up with this kind of supportive family relationships. Some of us did not get our needs met. We didn't feel loved or respected. So today, family does *not* feel like a place to ask for help.

Once we become adults, there are many times that our "family of origin" issues surface. A child's behavior might trigger an old memory or a feeling. If we are not careful, our reaction may be unintentionally hurtful.

In order to relate to children in healthy ways, we must make sure that we are doing the recovery work needed to heal the past. We don't always have the opportunity to do this directly with the people involved. But we can work hard to separate ourselves today from those previously hurtful times.

In addition to doing our own healing work, we can also

learn how to communicate effectively with children. We can learn about children's needs and set reasonable expectations for them. We can create a network of supportive friends who are there to help.

Doing Nothing   JULY 3

"So, whatcha doing?"

"Nothing, what are you doing?

Today, many of us find our lives scheduled to the max. We have daily routines of work, school, lessons, sports activities, homework, shopping, and other chores. Children who are accustomed to being on the move with a full schedule are sometimes the same children who are bored when there is *nothing* to do. There is never any "down time" to just *be*.

Doing nothing is valuable. During this unstructured time, we have the opportunity to exercise our creativity. We can let spontaneity guide us to our next activity. Or we can just take some time to think, imagine or plan.

Doing nothing *with* a child gives us a chance to just sit and talk. If you can't remember the last time you did this, you're way overdue!

Independence Day   JULY 4

Today we celebrate America's Independence. We actually have many occasions to celebrate a child's independence.

The first toddling steps as she learns to walk
Putting on shoes, all by himself
Holding the dog's leash
Going off to kindergarten
Being left home alone
Learning to drive

We encourage independence when we offer choices and include children in some of our decision making. They also become more competent with experiments with self-care – dressing, brushing teeth, showering and washing hair, learning to cook, doing chores.

It can be hard to let go of our need to take care of them. But, someday, each child will venture out into the world. That first truly independent step will be easier if we have supported the learning needed along the way.

Positive Self-Talk for Parents JULY 5

It is so easy to let the negative tapes run in our heads.

That was stupid.

I don't have time to take care of myself.

These children are impossible!

We put ourselves down and let our feelings of guilt and inadequacy dominate. But, we don't have to just sit back and accept these voices. We can counter the negativity with reassuring, positive messages.

We can create our own positive affirmations based on our experiences and needs. These messages can be used during a moment of doubt. Or, they can be read several times daily to keep the negative thoughts away.

I can calmly respond to children's behavior.

This child's needs are number one.

I deserve to take care of myself.

Children need adults who are healthy and
    rested.

I can communicate what I need and want.

Love is at the heart of my interactions.

We can communicate positive messages to ourselves that give us support to be the best we can be.

You Have What You Need JULY 6

Especially on challenging days, we wonder if we can do anything right. But, we do have abilities that will serve us well. We have experiences which help us understand children. We just need to remember to use what we know.

We can *observe children*. We know them better than we sometimes realize. We know their likes and dislikes. We understand what certain behaviors mean.

We *love them*. We want the best for them and make choices and decisions based on that love.

We *can learn*. We can be open to trying new things. As children grow, we can, too.

We can *be patient*. Learning takes time.

We have *an enduring commitment*. We're here for them for the long haul.

We have what we need: love, understanding, patience, and commitment.

Yet

It takes time. Learning, growing, and figuring things out...they all take time. When children are frustrated, a gentle reminder can be soothing, encouraging the child to be patient:

> You don't know how to ride your bike – yet.
> You haven't learned your times tables – yet.
> You're not tall enough to ride the bumper cars alone – yet.

We need the same encouragement. As children grow we sometimes become frustrated with our inability to understand this new stage. Guiding children is based on trial and error. We try, learn, and try again.

> I don't know how to do bedtimes without a fight – yet.
> I don't know what these cries mean – yet.
> I haven't learned how to juggle work and family – yet.

Patience and practice can counter perfectionism. We will not get it just right without lots of effort. And besides, once we think we have figured everything out, something changes and we have to try again.

"Not yet" means there is hope. We can help children try again with patience, realizing there is still time for both of us to learn something new.

I Wonder! JULY 8

Watch a young toddler squatting on the sidewalk. She has been captivated by something. With an intense curiosity she inspects a pebble or a plant or maybe a passing beetle.

I wonder!

Taking apart an old radio, he inspects wires, transistors, speakers, and more wires. How does this work? Why doesn't it work any longer?

I wonder!

Stomping through the puddles, he is watching to see how far he can make the water splash.

I wonder!

Because so much is new in their eyes, they see with awe and wonder. What can we learn from children?

I wonder!

Choosing from the Menu JULY 9

Eating out can be a major hassle, screaming around the table, poor service, impatient adults, and squirmy children. Or, it can be a delight because the atmosphere is enjoyable, the service is wonderful, and we all get to choose exactly what we want. We laugh together and savor our own favorite foods.

Life is like this. Sometimes there are complications, hassles, and disagreements. At other times, we get to pick from a menu of choices and order exactly what we want. No matter what comes our way, we can appreciate the experience so much more if we are prepared to maintain a positive attitude.

We do have choices. We can decide how we will respond. We can show children how to be more accepting. We can consider each child's interests and help them decide what they really need right now.

Curses!

Sometimes the words that come out of a child's mouth are shocking. Preschoolers and young school-aged children are experimenting with language and may not even know what the word means. Teens often swear during interactions with friends.

Children are mimics. They copy us, reflecting everything they see and hear. When young children swear, the first thing we need to do is consider where they are hearing this. The language in our home or social environment is not always the influence we want for children. So, the first step is to clean up the environment.

When a very young child is using inappropriate words, it is often best to ignore it. The more attention we give to this behavior, the more the child is likely to repeat it. We can explain to older children that certain words are disrespectful or mean. "When you use mean words I can't help you. When you talk with kind words, I can." And then leave and try to ignore the child.

Remember to catch them *being good*. "I am glad to see you and Steven playing together and having fun." We can model appropriate language and encourage children to speak respectfully.

Letting Go of the Clutter

Clutter is all that stuff that we collect. It fills every nook and cranny and overflows onto all the counters and floors. Even if we promised ourselves we would not get too many toys, before we know it, there's just too much!

Children grow up and grow out of old toys. But, as soon as we try to give them away, old favorites become current favorites, again. Sorting through old toys together is an opportunity to teach children about generosity. What are they willing to share with someone else? We can also use this time to celebrate their growth and new skills. We can help them realize that while they still like this toy a little, a younger child would like it a lot, as they once did.

Sometimes we feel emotionally attached to their childhood treasures. They remind us of precious times. This letting go is as much our rite of passage as it is theirs. We can model letting go. If you don't use it, if it no longer brings you pleasure and joy, pass it on!

I Only Want Purple!! JULY 12

We all have preferences. We have favorites. We have favorite foods. We have preferences for the kinds of clothes we wear and the colors we like. We have our own ideas about what kinds of activities we enjoy. Not everyone likes the same television shows or movies.

The challenge comes as we try to find a way for peaceful coexistence. This is not always easy, because we live with people who all have their *own* ideas about things.

We can learn to let go. Some things just really aren't worth fighting about. Is it really *that* important whether she wears her favorite, soft purple sweater or the new red one? It *is* important to her and you can avoid an unnecessary fight.

If you are going to get a picture taken, you can take his favorite shirt along with you so he can change into it right after the sitting. You can also ask the photographer to take one with his favorite shirt, too. When you look back, you will probably smile more with memories of his strong preferences.

We can't always get our way. But, hopefully, we can *all* have our choice, at least sometimes.

"Mine!"

Children learn generosity. But, sharing is not easy. They want to have all of the toys. They want to play the game their way! They need to feel they have control of the situation.

We do not always model generosity for children. We have some things which we are not comfortable sharing, like our car or special books. So, it is not realistic to expect children to be willing to share *all* of their special treasures either. If they are going to have friends over, we can minimize some of the disputes which naturally arise over toys by putting a few away.

> "Tommy is coming over to play. You can choose four things to put away that you are not willing to share. Then, I would like you to promise to share everything else. Do we agree?"

We can create a cooperative environment where we work together and share. We can honor every person's right to have a few special, private things. We can also make sure to acknowledge generosity and kindness when we see it.

"Why?"

Children have an amazing natural curiosity. Before learning to talk, they explore with all their senses. They look at an object, turning it over, tasting it, trying to figure out what it does and how it works. They learn with their whole body as they crawl, creep, reach for, grab, and taste. As language emerges, they try on words as they realize the power they gain through verbal communication.

By around age two, the "Whys" start. They are curious about everything. They want to understand.

> "It's time for dinner." "Why?"
> "Let's get ready to take a walk." "Why?"
> "Time to clean up and get ready for bed."
>   "Why?"

With each answer we offer, there is another "Why?"

Though answering questions can help encourage curiosity, we don't need to play a non-stop Why-game. After a few attempts to satisfy this child's curiosity, we can respond with, "I've given you my idea. What do you think?" Often, there isn't an absolute answer. So whatever the child's response, we can follow up with, "That's an interesting idea." Children deserve honest answers. When we respond to their questions, we are encouraging their curiosity.

The New Baby
JULY 15

> "There's a new baby in our house."

This is a joyous event. But, the new baby is not always greeted with pleasure. Sometimes older siblings feel left out when baby gets constant attention. The age difference between the children can influence a child's reaction, but there is always some kind of adjustment to life with a new family member.

To better understand a child's reaction, imagine for a moment that one day your partner brought home another spouse. "I just thought we had enough love to be able to share it with this person, too."

Does anything else need to be said? In a situation like this, most of us adults would feel jealous, angry, hurt, scared, and displaced. Is it any wonder that children sometimes feel this way, too? In fact, it's a miracle when the new baby is accepted willingly and lovingly!

We can do our best to prepare children for the arrival of a brother or sister. And, we can accept that this transition will take some patience as we all adjust to life with one more.

Raising a Son
JULY 16

> "Sticks and snails and puppy dog tails,
> that's what little boys are made of."

> "Boys will be boys."

Boys are actually just as different from each other as they

are alike. They have their own feelings. They have their own interests and abilities. They do well with some things and have a hard time with others. Some like sports, some prefer inside play. Some are very mechanical and love to take things apart and put things together. Others have no interest at all in how things work.

Each boy is a unique individual. In order to grow to his fullest potential, a boy needs –

> *Positive adult role models* who set good examples.
>
> Opportunities for *learning to be nurturing, kind, and caring* so that they will become good brothers, uncles, husbands, and fathers.
>
> Lessons in *solving conflicts without using fists.*
>
> *Good friends* to hang out with and share interests.
>
> *Time* to develop his talents and follow his dreams.

Raising a son is not really very different from raising a daughter. All children need adults who love them. They need adults who notice what helps them grow and thrive. They need adults who are there for them, listen to them, and share their lives.

Raising a Daughter   JULY 17

> "Sugar and spice and everything nice,
> That's what little girls are made of."

All children are influenced by the expectations of those around them. Some adults expect girls to always be sweet and act like a lady. Others expect girls to fight to be the best.

The media presents unrealistic standards of beauty, which girls can all too quickly adopt. They may strive for unreachable physical perfection or feel hopelessly left out by their sense of ordinariness.

Some girls are very social and excel in relationships. Others are much more comfortable with solitary entertainments. We can encourage girls to strive for balance as they make independent decisions or work together with others where appropriate.

Girls are actually as different from each other as they are from boys. We can counteract narrow gender stereotypes. Being encouraged to take reasonable risks is vital for girls to learn how to make choices and deal with the consequences. We help both boys and girls when we ask them to help out, no matter what the chore.

Each child is a unique mix of personality traits, talents, abilities, and strengths. All children need strong adult role models who reflect their special abilities. Thankfully, girls can choose to be anything they want to be. We can do our best to help each child make choices that are right for them and be all that they are meant to be.

Sleepless Nights JULY 18

Probably one of the hardest times for parents is their children's restlessness in the middle of the night. Tired parents can become cranky and a little crazy with this sleep deprivation.

Children do not all have the same patterns for sleeping and waking. Some are night-owls from the start. They are up late and sleep late in the morning. Others need two naps for several years and don't outgrow a nap until they are about five years old. Others lose the need to nap by age two, only rarely falling asleep in their food at dinnertime.

Even when we do all the right things to encourage night-time routines, children still have their own internal clock. Some just require less sleep than we wish they did.

There will be sleepless nights over the years, as we anxiously await the sound of our teen's car pulling in. Sometimes we lie awake worrying about their safety. Eventually, children figure out sleep and many other things, on their own. So can we.

Follow Through

When children misbehave, a consequence is in order. We want them to learn that certain behaviors are not appropriate. But, if we don't follow through with an active response, they will learn that anything goes. They may not believe that we are serious unless we respond with a roar!

> "If you don't stop banging that toy, I'm going to take it away."

> Still banging the toy, we threaten again, but the behavior does not change.

> "If you do that one more time, I'm going to...."

Our tone of voice gets louder. Our threats become like a broken record, stuck on a scratch. Children learn to push and push until we finally react by giving in with a "whatever!" or blowing up.

If instead, we follow through immediately, children learn to take us seriously. They realize there are limits and rules.

> "If you can't play gently with that toy, we will need to put it away."

When we follow through, children learn to trust that we mean what we say.

Fighting Fire with Fire

Fighting doesn't work. If someone is upset and we join in with our own anger, it can be like adding fuel to a fire. Before we know it, the heat has intensified and the fire has grown into a blazing inferno. We rarely find a fair solution when feelings are this intense. So, when fighting with fire, someone usually gets burned. What do children learn from these kinds of encounters? The biggest or the loudest or the meanest wins.

With a more positive approach to conflict resolution, we can both win. We can negotiate an agreement, as we both bend a little to find a solution that will work for each of us.

Whether we are dealing with a toddler or a teen or another adult, we can work to make peace and find a reasonable solution.

First, we must cool the coals of anger. Take a few deep breaths. Take a walk or a time-out, if needed. Now, start fresh. Listen. Give each person a chance to speak and be heard. There is a better way!

Taking Sides   JULY 21

When children play together, there are often demands for assistance. They ask us to take sides. "It's his fault!" "No, she did it first!"

Be careful! It always takes two. Even when one child is more feisty and demanding, the quieter child often finds a subtle way to stir things up. Though it may not be intentional, it is no less annoying. If we step into the role of judge, children often shift their frustrations to us. We become the "bad guy."

In the long term, we want them to learn to deal with their own conflicts and resolve them peacefully. If little sister is getting into big brother's stuff, he must learn how to resolve this. Maybe he needs to keep his things picked up and his door closed. And if his sister has something he would like to play with, he needs to ask her if he can borrow it and offer her something else.

As long as no one is getting physically hurt, we can stand on the sidelines as a facilitator and assist them in doing their *own* problem solving.

"How You Gonna Make Me?"   JULY 22

Everyone wants to feel like they have some control over their lives. Children can be very resistant. They don't want to do anything we ask. Maybe she is busy doing something right now and our request is an interruption. Or it is something that does not interest her. Maybe it seems boring or hard. Some children are also very independent and don't want anyone to tell them what to do. They have their reasons for resisting.

We can respond by acknowledging the child's feelings –

"I know this is not your favorite activity, but we all need to work together."

We can offer choices that give children a sense of power, too –

"This needs to be done, but you can start on it now or in 20 minutes after you have finished what you're doing."

And though it can be challenging for us, children need to be able to stand up for themselves and say "No!" We want them to resist dangerous activities or poor choices that their peers may suggest. So, they need to practice standing up for themselves with us.

We can be firm when needed and say, "I know you don't want to do this, but it's important." We can gain cooperation through patience and respect.

Taking Responsibility   JULY 23

You've heard it: "I didn't do it. She did!" Or "Mom, he's bothering me again. I can't do my homework!" These comments suggest that it's someone else's fault. Adults *and* children play this game. We sometimes blame children for our headache when their noise and activity is too much for us. They blame us when they run out of time to play because we insisted they clean their room.

We are making many decisions for children. We decide on routines. We decide who will be our child care provider. We decide where we will go on a family vacation. Then toddlers begin to make some of their own choices about foods or toys, resisting whenever their preferences are different from ours.

We are making choices all the time. By school age, children are responsible for many of their own choices. We can reinforce this by responding,

"I hear you. It sounds like you did that because

you felt pressured to do what he wanted, even though you knew it was not safe. But, you are still responsible for your choices."

One of the tasks of growing up is learning to make healthy, safe choices and taking responsibility for the consequences.

Push Me – Pull You   JULY 24

In the classic children's book, Dr. Doolittle encounters an odd llama-like animal that is a perfect illustration of how we often feel about children's behavior. Where there should be a tail, the *Push Me – Pull You* has a second head on a second long neck. One head faces one direction and tries to pull all of the feet that way, while the other head tries to tug in the opposite direction.

Toddlers want to do things their own way, "Me do it!" The next minute, they melt in our arms, wishing to be held or wanting us to help them. The school-aged child wants to have the same privileges as big sister, but doesn't want to take responsibility for chores. Teens want us to get out of their lives, *after* we have driven them to the mall.

Growing up has difficult moments. There are so many choices and decisions to be made. There is often a strong desire for independence and an equally strong need to be loved, cherished, and cared for. Is it any wonder that we sometimes feel confused by their behavior?

Don't take it personally. Set clear limits. Eventually children will learn to walk on their own in the right direction for them.

Stuck in a Rut   JULY 25

Your habit has been to yell at your child's misbehavior and send her to her room. But, you just completed a class on effective discipline, and learned some new ways of responding. You want to deal with her behavior with more patience. But, habits can be hard to break. When you are feeling stressed out, you still yell, forgetting your new skills.

Or, sometimes children's behaviors demand that we take a second look. They have grown and changed. What may have been an appropriate action in the past no longer works. It's time to see this with fresh eyes.

This is what being "in a rut" is about. It takes effort, practice, and persistence to work our way out of that deep pattern and create a new habit.

We can take time to think before we react. We can slow down our response. And when we forget and slip back into the rut, we can forgive ourselves, apologize, and try again.

"You Can Do It!"

Everyone needs a pep talk once in a while –

> When we are going through changes and feel
>   overwhelmed;
> When new experiences are hard to swallow;
> When we don't have the energy for more thing;
> When we are trying to finish something
>   difficult.

It helps for someone to say, "I believe in you. You can do it!"

Words can sting or words can soothe. We can carefully craft our words to pass on loving messages which nurture a child's sense of confidence.

A supportive attitude is not delivered in words alone. Confidence is built over time with successful experiences. We can encourage children to try something new. They can learn to complete a task, one step at a time.

If we expect too little and do too much, children get the message that they can't do anything without us. If we expect too much, children are frustrated because they don't believe they have the skills to even try. Our realistic expectations make a difference.

Fingerprints on the Wall

Fingerprints on the walls, on the stove, on the window. Curious hands leave their mark. Grubby fingers are evidence that this child is too busy for washing. Also, children who are learning to walk or run steady themselves with any surface.

Fingerprints are unique, just as each child is unique. Did you know that there are no two people with the same fingerprints? Fingerprints are randomly created before we are born. Why? Scientists believe that they are friction ridges which give us the traction to hold objects. Imagine if your hands were smooth. Things would just slip out of your grasp.

Everything about our body is unique. No two organs are completely identical. Nature just isn't that precise. Each individual is at least slightly different from anyone else, physically and emotionally. Each child is unique, with unique needs, talents, and abilities.

Respect Is Earned

"I don't feel any respect. These
children just won't listen to me."

Many of us grew up with the notion that children "should be seen and not heard," "speak when spoken to," and "respect their elders." This kind of respect was actually more about fear and anxiety. Respect meant control. Children were taught to fear the possible consequences of disobedience. Sometimes children even got the message that they were not valued and appreciated unless they were quiet and obedient. They had very little say in their lives.

Feelings of "respect" are actually learned through experiences of trust and security. Respect requires a mutual relationship in which adults give as much respect for children and their needs as they get back in love and cooperation. Genuine respect is earned.

Unconditional Love

No matter what!

"There is absolutely nothing that my children
could do that would ever diminish my deep love
for them."

But in spite of our best intentions, our love is sometimes
communicated with "strings" attached.

I love you –

When you get your homework done.

When you respond to my request.

When you play nicely with your sister.

When you go to bed and stay in bed.

Children need regular assurance of our love. Even when
things are not going well, these assurances count the most!

I love you –

Even when you and your brother are
fighting.

Even when you are angry at me.

Even when you refuse to help out.

Even when I disapprove of your decisions.

Children Need a Compass

How would we get to our destination without a road
map? How could we even read the road map if we didn't
have a sense of direction? We need to know where we are
going and how to get there.

Children need a compass. A compass tells us where to
turn. A compass tells us what's right. For children, we provide a compass when we set limits. A compass establishes
right and wrong. Without a compass, children get lost.

Children want to do the right thing. They are naturally
curious and energetic. When they are young, their impulses
can take them down wrong turns as they follow their curiosity. Children need supportive adults who lovingly guide them

and show them the way.

A compass is consistent. North is always North. We need to be consistent, too. Although the rules flex as children grow and become more competent, our loving presence is at the root of our guiding direction.

The Wind in Our Sails

JULY 31

What puts the wind in our sails? Where do we find the spirit to move forward? What serves to motivate us to stick with a difficult project or try new things?

> *Excitement* – This is fun!
> *Anticipation* – We look forward to the future.
> *Wonder and awe* – Children remind us every
>   day.
> *Grit and determination* – Just hang in there!
> *Curiosity* – What will happen if I do this?

Children sometimes provide all the encouragement we need. We want the very best for them. We want them to have the opportunities which will help them do well in life. Their confidence in us is like a burst of wind in *our* sails when we are feeling frustrated. We try harder for their sakes. We accomplish things to make life better for them and for us, like going back to finish school.

We can also be an encouraging breeze for children. We show our support by gently saying, "Come on, give it a try. I bet you can do it."

August

Reflections

Children are always learning, especially when we don't really mean to teach –

> We see a child shaking a finger at a doll, shouting, "No! No!"
>
> We hear children repeat swear words that slip out of our mouths all too often and all too easily.
>
> Children say, "Be quiet! I'm watching my show."
>
> To get your attention, he interrupts with, "I need you to stop that and do this right now."

We hear our own words and see our gestures in their responses. "Do what I say, and not what I do." It just doesn't work that way. They mimic what we say AND what we do. We never really get a break from their watchful eyes and sensitive ears. So, we have a responsibility to model what we want from them.

Children's behaviors can serve as a mirror for us. Their behavior reminds us that we need to be careful so that their behavior reflects our love, our patience, and our interested attention.

Change Is Expected

As children learn something new, we can expect to see shifts in other areas. A simple example is when a toddler learns to walk. The world opens up! There are now so many choices to explore. They are excited one minute and very frustrated the next.

The new walker feels a greater sense of control, and wants even more. Power struggles come up where there were none. This busy toddler now communicates with her feet, making her own decisions about the things she wants to play with and running away from people or activities she wants to avoid. Relationships take on new meaning.

Routines can shift as well. On the go, he may not be hungry. Or spending extra energy moving, he may want to eat more often. Sleep is also much less dependable.

Whether we are talking about a child moving on to the next grade in school, a teen starting to date, or even ourselves facing a life change, development in one area naturally brings shifts in others. What can we count on? Change! Our openness and flexibility help smooth the transition.

Heart Felt   AUGUST 3

When children hurt, we hurt. When things are going well, we rejoice with them. The joy is much easier than the pain! Is this ever going to end? Will we ever be able to let go of the pain of seeing our child frustrated and overwhelmed by difficult experiences? Will we ever be able to let go of our need to fix it, to kiss it and make it all better?

Yes, children need to learn to resolve conflict and challenges independently. We can express our confidence, and hope that they will feel inspired by this, too.

"I know you can do this. I trust that you have
what you need to find a solution for this."

We also need to believe what we say to them. We need to trust each child's development. Children do grow up. They learn how to make their own way in the world. We can offer our support and advice, and our blessings for the journey.

Outside the Box   AUGUST 4

We'd like everything to be neat and tidy, but life rarely is. There can be many happy moments, but it can also be messy and difficult. We don't always have the support we need. We are not always prepared for the new experiences that children seem to be ready to leap into. And leap they must – into the first day at a new school, staying overnight at a friend's for the first time, or learning to read.

We also learn to step outside of our comfort zone and try

new things. Learning is limited from inside the box. Inside are all those things we have come to count on, where things don't change.

Thinking and acting *outside the box*, children gain confidence, learn new skills, practice making choices and decisions, and meet new people. Alongside them, we can learn to trust the possibilities out there, and remember that growth is happening, especially *outside the box.*

You Gotta Love 'Em! AUGUST 5

Sometimes children are easy to love. They are so precious, cute, helpful, and considerate! Other times, loving them is more challenging. They are into everything. They forget what we asked them to do. They snap at us with a sassy complaint.

But, hey, you gotta love 'em –

> When he complains about doing his chores,
> but does them anyway.
> When they bicker with each other about which
> TV show to watch...and figure it out.
> When she surprises you with a flower from
> someone's garden.
> When he shows kindness toward a neighbor.
> When they are belted into their seats ready to
> go.

The reasons are many! You just gotta love 'em!

Kid-Friendly Vacations AUGUST 6

Are we having fun yet? Will this time away really be restful? With reasonable expectations, we can have a good time. Vacations can be fun and relaxing, especially when they are kid-friendly.

Include children in the planning when possible. Think about what would make the vacation fun for them. Bring along some easily portable toys and activities. There are special games that can be saved for long car trips. Children also like having their own player and earphones to listen to their favorite music, movie, or story tapes.

When vacations involve driving long distances, be sure to have frequent breaks. Find places along the way where they can run and play. Stop to get snacks or to have a picnic.

Relax! Routines will be thrown way off, but this easing of structure can be fun. Slow down. Enjoy the trip.

A Change of Pace

We all need a break. Sometimes too much of a good time is still TOO much. Maybe we have just had too much together time. And we are driving each other nuts. Siblings and friends, children and adults can definitely get on each other's nerves.

How can we adjust this situation to change the energy? What can we do to give each other a break? We need a change of pace. Sometimes a new activity or a new person can make all the difference.

Inviting another child over can help, someone with a calm, agreeable personality. An older child or a willing teen can be invited to entertain the younger kids while we get some time to finish a project. One-on-one time between adult and child may also change the energy.

There are no magic solutions. Something that works one time may not the next. When it does work, store it away in the "bag of tricks" for next time. We can find creative ways to get a much needed break for ourselves and for others.

Finding a Stand-In

Whether we work outside the home or want to find someone to offer occasional respite, we need someone to help with child care. We need someone who will "stand in" for us and take caring for children seriously.

Whether we find a family member, a friend, or a licensed facility, turning the care of our child over to someone else

– even for a short time – can be very tough. "Can anyone else love my child the way I do?" More important than the cost and the location, we want to find a magical person – a *Wonder Woman* or *Super Man*.

Finding the right person can be challenging because we want the *very* best for our child. We want him to feel comfortable and safe. And we want to feel this way, too.

Even with our concerns and expectations, finding the right person to help us out is possible. Someone is available right now who can offer love and support to our child when we are away.

"I Quit!" AUGUST 9

> "I hate this! Everything is a fight! I don't know what to do. How can I help my children? They are always at each other. The oldest teases the middle one. Then the middle one harasses the youngest. I am so sad and worried for them. Will they ever be friends?"

Sometimes we just want to give up! We are so tired of the endless conflicts. We just don't have any energy left to deal with this. But, deal with this we must. Children need our support to help them work through their conflicts. Our calm presence can have a soothing effect. And when they are demonstrating kindness and understanding, our acknowledgment can reinforce the positive behavior.

When we are rested, we have more patience. Then, rather than running away, we can say to ourselves,

> "I don't like this. I am uncomfortable with conflict. But, I can do this. I can be a positive support to my kids."

With self-care and positive self-talk, we are energized. Hang in there!

It's Cool to Stay Cool

In almost every conflict, there is a better way to respond. Realistically, when a child is reaching for something dangerous, a firm and strong reaction is necessary. We want our tone to literally stun him so that he freezes and avoids a potential calamity.

But most of the day-to-day conflicts do *not* involve major physical dangers. They are annoyances. Children test our authority and the rules we have set to maintain safety, respect, and a peaceful setting.

If all of our interactions are loud and negative, children learn to tune us out, thinking, "There she goes again." Instead, our interaction is more likely to be effective if we take a breath and stay cool. A calm response to a child's behavior says, "I respect you. I know you want to learn. We can work this out together."

Affirmations for Parents

Positive words of reassurance help us all. Adults are much less likely to hear them, so we can learn to give them to ourselves:

> I am a unique individual with gifts and talents.
> I can ask for the support and help that I need.
> I am giving myself and my children the love we deserve.
> I am doing the best I can. This is enough for today.
> I can do this.
> I can get through the hard times.
> I can give positive feedback to my kids.
> I can respond calmly to my child's request for help.
> I can tell my kids I need time to think about it.
> I am learning from my mistakes.

Responding with Love

Children sometimes say hurtful things.

"I hate you!"

"Daddy's my favorite."

"You're mean! You never let me stay up."

When the drama surfaces in these biting words, it is hard to stay neutral ourselves. We want to snap back, "Don't you talk to me that way!" But, if we do, we are adding fuel to a fire, fighting back with our own drama.

It's better to respond with love. "I know you're upset with me right now. I care about you even when you are mad or sad." Children need the reassurance that we love them, the whole package. We love their humor. We love their generosity. We love their creativity. We love their energy and enthusiasm. We love them when they make unhealthy choices. And we love them with all of their feelings.

We can strive to respond to every interaction with love.

Into the Deep End

Do you remember learning how to swim? At first it was a huge accomplishment to be able to hold your breath and put your face into the water. Then, head under the water, you counted up to 10 or 15 seconds. But your feet were still planted on the bottom of the pool with your head and shoulders well above the water.

The next step was to walk deeper into the water and learn to float or to paddle feet and hands to get to safety at the edge. Learning to swim becomes a reality in stages. Finally, children become confident and brave enough to jump into the deep end.

This experience mirrors many things a child will eventually accomplish. In the beginning, most things seem impossible to imagine. By the time the learning lightbulb goes on, it has become a very automatic activity.

Learning math

Becoming comfortable speaking in front of a
group
Learning to drive

Many things start out impossible, then, with experience, we become ready to jump into the deep end with confidence.

The Last Word

Guess what? You don't have to have the last word. You just need to follow through with what you last said. You ask her to do something:

"No, you're not my boss!"
"Oh yes, I am, and I say do it now!"
"No!" screaming and running away.

This war of words can escalate very quickly.

How can we deal with this differently? Before making your request, notice what she is doing and figure out the respectful way to interrupt. Gently get her attention and give a warning. "In ten minutes I need you to take a break from this activity and do something else."

When the time comes, go directly to her, get down at eye level, and make your request. Even when children come back at this point with yet another verbal volley, we can patiently point her in the desired direction.

We don't need a verbal comeback. We can let our patient, persistent behavior speak for itself.

Body Curiosity

It is normal for children to be curious about many things. When it comes to bodies, two-year-olds already have an uncanny ability to identify most shapes and sizes of adults by gender. Three- and four-year-olds have figured out the basic body parts and enjoy letting everyone know.

Not surprisingly, a child's personal body awareness progresses to being curious about all bodies. When children's play includes body curiosity, it's best to respond with open doors and close adult supervision. Children also need to be taught about body privacy. "This is your body. And your body is private. It is important to keep your hands to yourself."

We want children to develop a healthy relationship with their own body. So we must be careful to avoid body judgments about size or gender. Since children are curious and likely to ask questions, we need to examine our own comfort or concerns about talking about this issue. It is our job to answer a child's questions. When we are honest and direct, we help them feel comfortable, just as they are!

"I Messages"

With effective communication, we share our point of view and receive a response. We use words which open up the dialogue.

All of us have also spoken too quickly, without thinking about the effect our words will have on another. We have said hurtful things. One way we shut down communication is by using "You Messages." These statements threaten, blame, and direct:

> You shouldn't do that.
> You're such a brat!
> You're acting like a baby.
> You NEVER do that for me!

These statements do not create an atmosphere of cooperation. The recipient feels judged, unappreciated, incapable, and harassed.

"I Messages" honestly tell the other person (our child, sibling, friend, or co-worker) how we feel when we are frustrated and hurt or excited and pleased. We send a clear message of our feelings to the receiver. "I Messages" avoid accusation and encourage positive action.

> "I'm really tired. It would really help me to have a few minutes to myself, then we can spend

some time together doing what you want."

"I Messages" clearly communicate how we are feeling and what we need right now.

Oil and Water AUGUST 17

They don't mix. At times, it may feel like children don't mix, either. Everything is a fight. "Mom, he looked at me!" They won't play together. In fact, they rarely can be in the same room together without a blow-up.

Usually, this is temporary. Maybe this is a transition period, as each child experiences developmental challenges or growth spurts. We want children to get along. We want them to be supportive of each other, and protective, if the need arises.

Children can learn to negotiate their time together. One child may be very social and demand a great deal of interaction. If the other child needs more alone time, we can help them work out a compromise.

> "I know you want to spend time with your sister. How about you both do something together for 30 minutes. Then, you will both get 30 minutes of alone time to do your reading or whatever you want."

Children can learn to create peaceful time together. Even when they do not get along, we can still encourage an attitude of respect and cooperation.

Sharing Is Hard AUGUST 18

At what age do children learn to share? The answer is complicated. Toddlers do not know how to share. "Mine!" is a persistent cry when another toddler grabs a toy. Even if a "cherished" toy has not been played with for days, another child's interest can ignite a territorial dispute.

Usually by the time children are four years old, they can learn to negotiate and take turns. They usually want to play with others and work out fun agreements. If a friend is coming to visit, we can suggest that if there are a few special toys, these can be put aside to avoid any hassles.

Though older children have a greater capacity for cooperation, there are still some belongings that are hard to share, like a favorite toy or bicycle. Adults also have things we are unwilling to allow others to use, like our cars, jewelry, special books, or clothes. It helps us understand a child's reluctance to share treasures, when we remember that we do not always want to share either.

Once they understand the concept of ownership, most children become willing to share generously and give freely.

Instead of Spanking   AUGUST 19

There is *always* something else that can be done in response to misbehavior, instead of spanking. What does spanking say?

"I'm bigger than you are."

"Hurting is okay."

"This is the way we settle our disagreements."

If a child runs into a busy street, we must bring him safely to the curb, hug him tightly, then dramatically explain our fears. "Cars are dangerous and go fast. If you can't play on the sidewalk, you will need to play in the house."

If a child has just hit her little brother, we first make sure the injured child is okay, then separate the children. "It is not okay to hurt your brother. If you have a problem with what he is doing, tell him. If you need help, come get me."

If a child comes back at us with a sassy, rude comment, we can use words to describe our feelings. "I don't appreciate that disrespectful tone. When you are ready to talk calmly and politely, I am here to listen and work with you."

What do we want to teach children? Do we want them to be afraid of us and our angry reactions? Or do we want children to learn about respect and safety? Children learn best when we guide them with love and respect.

Finding Our Center

Aikido is a martial arts approach that provides a disciplined setting to help the students *find their center* and deflect negativity. By a series of balanced, flowing movements, an aggressor is skillfully thwarted.

Through this training, confidence is gained as the moves are mastered. Students become more comfortable working with others, touching appropriately, and communicating respectfully. Aikido is not just a physical discipline. It is also a way of life, as the trainees tap into the quiet at their center which allows them to focus, watch, and respond quickly.

Aikido principles can also serve us as we interact with children. How can I achieve a balance in my response to children? What would help me gain confidence in my guidance skills? How can I learn to flow effortlessly from one interaction to the next? What can I do to commit my time and efforts to working on understanding children and how to help them manage their own behavior?

When we respond from our center, our reactions are more respectful. We have more patience to listen. We are better able to determine what is really needed in any particular situation.

Becoming Responsible

We want children to learn how to make wise decisions and act responsibly. Toddlers and very young children do not have the reasoning ability they will eventually develop. They need clear limits for safety. Just saying "no" is not enough. They often need us to redirect them away from unacceptable behavior and show them what is safe and appropriate. "That's dangerous. Come over here and play with this."

When we offer limited choices to preschoolers, we are encouraging the beginnings of self-discipline. We are still clearly in charge. "Do you want to wear the red shirt or the blue shirt?" or "Would you like cereal or eggs for breakfast?"

School-aged children are ready for more responsibilities. They can place their dirty clothes into the hamper so that their favorite shirt will be washed, then fold their dry clothes and put them away. We can include them in weekly planning for chores and fun activities.

Children do not start out with the skills to be responsible and solve problems, but they are capable of learning.

Standing on Their Own AUGUST 22

Children will eventually stand on their own. Whether this is about learning to walk or making wise choices as a teen, we recognize their need for independence. But, we sometimes have trouble accepting what they have decided.

A mom had a heart-to-heart conversation with her pre-teen daughter and encouraged her to be sure to think for herself before going along with her girlfriends. Then, one day her daughter woke up and said she had decided she wanted to cut her lovely, long hair. Mom asked, "Have you checked with your friends about that yet?" Her daughter said, "Hey, Mom, I thought you said I should think for myself?"

Mom was not ready to let go of that lovely, long hair, but she laughed anyway and said, "You're right." Her daughter got her hair cut.

Children reach out and push the limits of their boundaries all the time. It is our job to be there for support, hold a hand if needed, and then know when it is time to let go!

Friend Choices AUGUST 23

We are not always comfortable with the friendship choices children make. And the quickest way to encourage a friendship is to voice our concerns and try to limit the interactions.

Children develop friendships based on fun and excitement, common interests, stimulating play, and availability. Sometimes the friend is just someone who lives nearby and is available to play.

We may be uncomfortable with a friend choice because of temperament issues. The friend may be impulsive and make unsafe decisions. A child who is a follower can be easily led to dangerous or inappropriate activities. Sometimes the personalities clash with intensity and we become tired of the constant negotiations required to resolve the social drama.

When we do have reasonable concerns, we can provide a supervised environment to allow for safe play. With a watchful eye, we can lend support when needed.

Empathy   AUGUST 24

You're exhausted. You haven't been feeling well and you flop into a chair, putting your feet up. In a matter of seconds, your heavy eyelids are drooping.

Up walks your toddler. "Mommy tired?" "Yes." He runs off toward his room and comes back a few minutes later dragging his favorite blanket. He does his best to cover you, "Mommy sleep." "Thank you, sweetie."

You realize this rest will probably be very short-lived. Maybe you can coax him into joining you. If you're really lucky, your toddler will fall asleep in your arms and you'll both get some much needed sleep.

No matter how old the child, these tender offerings are a true gift, often learned from you. "Thank you, sweetie."

Trusting Our Instincts   AUGUST 25

What is this child's behavior telling you she needs? Be careful. This question is very different from, "What do you *think* would be good for her right now?" Sometimes *our* own needs get mixed in and we lose sight of what is really best for children.

Taking the time to observe children helps us understand them. When we pay attention to their behaviors and reactions, we develop a deep knowing. We learn to read their body language. We feel it when she is upset, frustrated, tired, excited, worried, or pleased.

Over time, our experiences teach us that we can trust our own instincts about this child. Do we have innate instincts that automatically shift into gear? Probably not. Our instincts must be fine tuned and nurtured. We do this when we take the time to see the world through their eyes. We come to understand children by imagining what it is like from their perspective.

Eventually, we trust what we know. Then, when children struggle, we are ready to respond with understanding and support.

Baby Steps   AUGUST 26

Nothing really happens overnight. We actually go through life-transforming changes one baby step at a time.

Sometimes we refuse to try something new because we believe it will take too long to figure it out. We don't have the patience or the time. This attitude gets us nowhere. It is especially sad when children pick this up from us. They, too, become stuck in familiar habits, afraid to try new things. They don't even want to take safe, reasonable risks.

We are all learning every day. Every day we can become one step closer to reaching our potential. But, we don't see important life lessons or understand their value unless we are open and willing to try.

When a baby is learning to walk, there are many stops and starts. If the baby were to just sit down, the world of possibilities would stop, too. By trying again, finally the child masters the balance and is able to take off! And the world opens up.

Winning the Race   AUGUST 27

Does it feel like you are in a long distance marathon? Each day can feel exhausting. Where is the finish line? How are we ever going to make it? Helping children reach adulthood requires preparation, patience, and persistence!

Racers have a clear goal. Ours is to help children develop

physical and emotional well-being leading to eventual adulthood. With our support and assistance, children can learn what they will need to be successful.

Physical preparation helps us go the distance. To have endurance, we must train adequately. We must eat right, get plenty of sleep, and keep fit. Classes and support groups can also be part of our fitness regime. Our good example is the best training advice we can give to children.

Patience and persistence will help us leap over hurdles along the way. When we believe in ourselves and children, no obstacle is too hard or too high.

Winning a race or accomplishing an important goal is supported by good coaching. All champions actually have a team of assistants. We can learn to accept help, too.

Little White Lies *AUGUST 28*

We do it all the time. The phone rings and we say, "Tell them I'm not here," when we really are. Or, "Tell her I am in the shower," if you're not even home. Or, you said you would do something, but you don't get to it.

Sometimes it's the little things that are the strongest influences. Children are watching us. When they are about five, they begin to create their own sometimes elaborate stories to explain their behavior or protect themselves from possible consequences.

Our honest responses and requests model the importance of the truth. This won't necessarily stop children from becoming creative, self-protective storytellers. But when you encourage a child to bravely admit the truth, you can do this with integrity. You will know that you are setting a positive example, valuing and demonstrating the importance of honesty, even with the little things.

Be Open to Receiving *AUGUST 29*

Being a care giver to children is hard work. We are on the giving end of the relationship much of the time. Sometimes we are so busy with daily demands that we miss some of the surprising developments going on right in front of us.

Our relationship with children is reciprocal. We both give *and* receive. When we are paying attention, we can see children grow and learn. We can see and hear and touch the magic opening up before us. Children offer us gifts that come in many packages –

> We hear the wisdom from the mouths of babes!
> We notice when a child figures something out!
> We observe a polite response from an other-
> wise boisterous child!
> We receive many hugs and *thank yous!*

If we watch, if we listen, if we give our best, if we wait... we receive so much more back from children than we ever imagined.

A New School Year AUGUST 30

Ready, Set, Go! Children greet the new school year with mixed emotions. Some are excited. Others feel shaky and scared. All children ask themselves questions – What will my new teacher be like? Will some of my friends be in my class? What will the classroom look like? Will I like the school lunches? Will we have long enough recesses? Whether a kindergartner or a senior in high school, children wonder what this new school year will be like.

Parents and teachers can support this transition by realizing that children adapt in their own ways, and at their own pace. When the territory is unfamiliar, they feel awkward. Anything we do to allow them to ease into this new setting can help them make a smoother adjustment.

Talking about a typical day can help prepare the child. Sharing stories from our childhood may also help. Consistent routines and a light schedule in the early weeks can also make for an easier adjustment to the new school year.

Some children jump right in. Some do not. Sometimes, we are the ones who are most challenged by these new experiences. No matter what, preparation and understanding can help to smooth this transition.

Interrupting *August 31*

Children can be taught to interrupt respectfully. This begins with our own behavior. What do we do to get a child's attention? We often interrupt them without noticing what they may be in the middle of, as if what they are doing is not as important as our request. We interrupt from across a room or even a different room by raising our voice and demanding immediate attention.

Children can be taught a gentle interruption technique. We can ask them to go up to the adult and without saying a word, to rest their hand gently on the adult's arm. Then the adult can give an immediate response in one of several ways:

> "Yes, how can I help you?" or "What do you need?" (if it is convenient to stop what you're doing)

> "Wait just a minute, let me finish this conversation first." (being sure to keep the wait short)

It goes both ways. We can remember to respectfully get a child's attention. When we want a child's attention, we can come up beside him and without saying a word, rest our hand gently on his arm and wait for a response. When he looks up or says something, we can make our request.

September

Comfort Zone

All of us find it easier to function and cope when we are in our "comfort zone." Children look to parents and other adults for reassurance. Children find comfort in...

Feeling loved and cared for.

Routines and limits – they appreciate knowing
what to expect.

Being listened to – they want to talk about their
day and what they are doing.

Play where they can work out their feelings and
practice real life situations.

Being helpful.

Hugs and the healing power of touch.

As we all make the transition from summer to the school year, remember that children sometimes have a hard time with change. With time, they again find their "comfort zone."

Hurry Up and Slow Down

We are in a hurry!

"Come on! Get dressed! We've got to go now or
we'll be late!"

"Stop fooling around and do your homework!"

Children can be confused by our hurried lifestyles. We rush through traffic, then squeeze in front of the next car, only to get off at the next freeway exit and have to stop at the light. We hurry to get to an appointment, just to wait in line for a long time.

We sometimes push. We are eager for children to walk. We look forward to the day when chores are completed without a reminder. At the same time, we may want their development to slow down. It sometimes seems their childhood is slipping away too quickly.

There are countless examples of "hurry up" in our daily

lives. We usually have a much harder time with slowing down. But slow down we must, and very soon, or we may miss some of the wonders of development. We need to take time to enjoy children now.

At some time in the distant future, we will *not* look back and wish we had driven faster to get to that appointment. But, we may wish we had spent more time playing with children.

We do need to hurry up – right now – and slow down. Slow down to cherish the moments.

Getting Out the Door SEPTEMBER 3

Mornings feel impossible sometimes. We may even be chronically late because there is just way too much to do before leaving home.

We can create morning routines to smooth out this regular hassle. The night before, look at your calendar and prepare for your day. Where are you going? What will be expected of you? What should you wear? Then, when you get up in the morning, you have already planned for the day.

Once you are dressed and ready, you can quietly and lovingly wake your children. If you take time the night before to also decide what they will wear and what they need to remember to take along, then the morning can go more smoothly for them, too. As a part of the bedtime routine, make sure their shoes, lunches, homework, and backpacks are by the door. Now they can grab them as they head out.

We really can start the day with less frantic screaming and complaining and much more positive attitudes. We really can get there on time.

Quality Time SEPTEMBER 4

With all the expectations on our shoulders, how can we ever find the time to be with our children? Well, we *do* have the time. We *can* take the time. Children reap the benefits when we make the commitment to engage in positive interactions with them.

Quality time is not about the amount of time we spend. We can have quality moments. They all add up. Even a trip to the store can be quality time if the car radio is off and we have an opportunity for an intimate conversation.

Quality time includes focused attention. Then children know that our time is theirs. We will not allow interruptions from phones or chores. Instead, we direct our energies toward them and what they want to do.

Quality time includes genuine listening. When we give eye contact and acknowledge with appropriate responses and body language, children feel heard.

Quality time includes pleasure and fun.

These precious moments can be planned. And we can also grab a moment of connection when it magically appears.

I Count When... SEPTEMBER 5

> I finish my homework.
> I am kind to my sister.
> I clean up my room.
> I help with dinner and set the table.
> I am quiet and listen to my mom.
> I comb my hair and dress right.
> I stop biting my nails.

There are many things we ask children to do. Let's be honest. We nag! Getting children to follow through is one of our biggest challenges. When they do, we need to remember to let them know we appreciate this.

Sometimes children get the impression that they *only* matter when they are doing the *right* thing. We need to give them the message that they count with us...no matter what! They are important to us when they are happy or sad, kind or angry, helpful, or resistant. We want the best for them. They need to understand that nothing they can do or say can change our enduring love for them.

Children always count with us!

Kindergarten

As children go to kindergarten, we recognize, sometimes with tears in our eyes, that this is an important rite of passage. They have learned many things to become ready for this moment. We have observed increased coordination, an amazing memory, budding knowledge of many things, and the steady expansion of their independence.

Once they enter kindergarten, the world will open up even more. They will learn many new concepts and gain abilities that will take them further along this developmental path. What will they learn?

> How to work cooperatively with others
> The importance of taking turns
> Increased coordination
> When it is important to pay attention
> The words and music to many songs
> The usefulness of numbers and letters
> Following directions
> And much more

It's time to celebrate! Kindergarten marks one of many steps toward growing up.

We're All in Recovery

No one escapes childhood without wounds. Some experiences have little impact, while others are significant:

> Friendships which broke up
> Constant teasing from peers
> Our parents' divorce
> Illness in the family
> Unreasonable responsibilities
> Poor choices
> Learning and school challenges

No matter what our experiences, we are often left with hurt, disappointment, sadness, and anger. The need for healing from these childhood experiences is important. Otherwise, the feelings left over from childhood continue to affect us today.

Recovery is a lifetime process. When we are stressed, we are more likely to react automatically, responding with old habits. When we continue to work on our issues from the past, we learn better ways to stay in the present and deal honestly with friends and loved ones.

Children benefit when we continue to deal with the wounds from our past. Now we can interact with them today in healthy ways.

Do Your Best

> Your daughter is trying to tie her shoes. She is feeling frustrated and can't seem to figure it out.
> Your son is tackling a really tough assignment. He doesn't understand the math and is feeling really stupid (his word).

No matter what the task might be, we hope they will do their best. Though we mean well, children sometimes receive the statement to "do your best" very differently than we intended. For some, this expectation feels like pressure and teaches a perfectionist attitude. Others receive it more simply as "give it a try."

We want children to try and give it some effort. We want to encourage a spirit of experimentation. Some people are motivated by a little encouragement. Others feel pressured. Then a sense of inertia takes hold and nothing gets done.

We can't really teach children to be patient when they are learning something new. But, we can avoid adding more unnecessary pressure. Children already have their own internal critics judging each new step. That inner voice is planted by the adults in their lives.

> "Come on, give it a try. And I'm right here if you need any help."

> *Caution – this behavior may be*
> *hazardous to a child's health.*

Children need watchful adults who observe from a reasonable distance. They need encouragement to empower them to try new things. They need to know, "I believe you can do this!"

But if we stand over them and interfere in many of their decisions, they get a very different message from us. They might think, "You can't do this on your own." Then when someone asks them to help with chores or to fix their own snack, their response is, "I can't!" They have no confidence in their own ability.

Other children become spoiled by the constant care of those who do everything for them. Their response might be, "I won't and you can't make me!" Still others will fight for independence and push over-protective adults away. They may have a hard time asking for help when they really need it. They are tired of the constant attention and want to be left alone!

Our job is to learn to support from a reasonable distance.

This, Too, Will Pass   SEPTEMBER 10

Sometimes it seems like someone came along and switched children with us during the night. This sweet, agreeable child has become demanding and defiant. Growing up is hard, stressful work.

Children's bodies are growing. They may feel more clumsy and awkward. Sometimes there are aches and pains which come along with the growth. No wonder they feel a little grumpy.

Children are also learning new social skills. They are learning how to be a friend. They are learning about rules and routines. They are learning about manners and appropriate behaviors in various settings. So, they may feel a little confused and sad.

Children learn thousands of concepts and ideas which help them read, write, do math, remember facts, and take care of themselves. Some find a new concept very easy to understand, while others struggle. Their brains are working full time to store all of this information. No wonder they sometimes feel overwhelmed.

When children are growing and learning new things, there are often ripple effects in other areas of their lives. Sleep and eating routines may shift. Emotional well-being may become shaky. Learning and growing can be very challenging. With our understanding, these difficult times will pass.

Believing in Them SEPTEMBER 11

When someone believes in us, truly believes in us, it feels like a warm coat on a cold day. We are all much more likely to succeed at whatever we attempt when we feel people are behind us cheering us on. When someone believes in us, we carry their love and support with us in whatever we do. They become the encouraging voices in our head during hard times.

Saying "I believe in you" means we have faith that all will unfold as life progresses. Saying "I believe in you" means we trust children to figure out what is important. "I believe in you" says we know in our hearts that children can create the life they need and want.

No matter what we might believe is possible, it isn't really possible for them until they trust deep inside that life is full of potential. So, we must leave messages of hope. Our optimistic attitude can help children believe in themselves and a future full of possibilities.

Appropriate Praise SEPTEMBER 12

Everyone needs encouragement. We all appreciate recognition when we have done something well. The most important part of our acknowledgment is how the other person feels inside as a result of our words. Sometimes our well-intentioned words can be met with rejection. We want children to realize that we noticed their good deed. Instead, they feel judged.

"You're always such a good helper."

Internal – "No I'm not. I hate doing this."

There are ways to communicate our appreciation that are more likely to lead to supportive internal messages. We can keep it simple and specific.

"Thank you for putting your dishes in the dishwasher."

Internal – "I was helpful."

"You and your brother seem to be having fun."

Internal – "Hmm, we are playing together."

We can offer affirmations that let children know that we notice their positive efforts.

A Resilient Spirit   SEPTEMBER 13

Everyone has the capacity to bounce back. Hard times happen. We face challenges and get through them. Adults who have overcome major personal challenges consistently report four qualities which helped them overcome adversity:

Resilient individuals have had *caring adults* during their growing years who openly showed their love and acceptance unconditionally – "I believe in you."

Resilient individuals are encouraged with *reachable expectations*. A supportive person says, "I believe you can do it."

Resilient individuals often have *opportunities to help others*. They are entrusted with a task which implies, "I trust you to do this."

Resilient individuals have *hope*. They believe they are part of something bigger and have a vision for the future.

There are experiences that limit and hinder our resiliency. But, caring adults who are available to children can help prepare the way to a successful future. We can help children overcome setbacks and develop the skills needed to recover and thrive.

Good Manners   SEPTEMBER 14

"The kids today are so disrespectful!"

Let's consider how children are treated –

"Hurry up. It's time to go!"

"Stop it. You're being such a brat!"

We want them to be respectful. But, where do they learn about respect? Are we treating them with patience and kindness? If we want children to be polite, we need to be polite to them.

"Thank you for helping put the dishes in the sink."

We ask them to wait during an appointment and expect them to be quiet and polite. Is this realistic? We don't want children to interrupt us when we are talking on the phone, but we interrupt them often to move them along to our next activity. We hope children will avoid swearing and yelling. But, do they hear us doing this?

Good manners and polite behavior are learned. The most powerful lessons come from the examples given by the adults in their lives.

Gentle Reminders   SEPTEMBER 15

Whenever we assume children will finish something on their own, without us first checking in with them, we are stepping into a potential misunderstanding. Our assumptions can get us into trouble.

We may think – "He knows how important it is

to feed the pets on time. We've talked about this often. He needs to remember this and take care of them without my nagging."

Instead of assuming something will happen and criticizing when it doesn't, we can give a gentle reminder. This is not nagging.

"Please take a break from what you're doing and feed the cat. Thank you."

When children surprise us and do a chore without our insistence, this is a perfect time to acknowledge the helpfulness –

"Thank you for remembering to feed the cat. I'm sure Sammy appreciates you."

It's not anyone's intention to forget. Gentle reminders help us stay on track.

The Choice Is Theirs SEPTEMBER 16

We do have a great deal of influence when children are young. But as they get older, it is natural and expected that children will begin to question adult authority, including their parents and teachers. Even a four-year-old will say, "You're not my boss!"

As children get older, they look at the world around them and see the contradictions. They question right and wrong. They test their boundaries and limits. If we want them to become independent, responsible adults, we will accept their need to make many of their own decisions.

Choosing along the way is just one thing that children must do to learn the tools for independence. They choose –

What they wear

How hard they work on homework or hobbies

Who their friends are

Whether they want to participate in an activity

When they are young, we offer choices. Soon they are making their own choices on the road to adulthood.

Children learn to hide their feelings. They learn to keep them inside when we say things like –

"It's not so bad, cheer up!"
"Don't you be angry at me!"
"Come on, you're a big girl."

Some children hide their true feelings behind laughter. Some hide behind busy-ness and activity. Some hide behind anger.

We can help children admit their pain and give them a chance to deal with their feelings in healthy ways. An important first step is to acknowledge their feelings. Then we can offer to help them figure out how to resolve their difficulty.

"I can tell you're disappointed. Want to talk about it?"

Or

"I'll bet you feel left out. What would be helpful for you right now?"

Feelings give us information that helps us understand. Rather than hide our feelings, we need to bring them into the open. Then, the challenge for all of us is to respond with appropriate words and actions.

First Class

Have you ever flown first class? For most people this is out of reach or at the very least, a rare treat. In first class, you sit in a soft chair with plenty of leg room. You are brought a warm wash cloth for your hands and face. You are served the food in courses and use real silverware.

Don't we all deserve to be given first class treatment? Our families deserve first class. We show them first class treatment when –

We respond with patience and calmness.
We offer our respect in all situations.
We listen with an open mind and heart.

We help them overcome their frustrations and
deal with challenging experiences.

Where there is a sense of panic, we can relax and accept
that everything will work out okay. Where there is fear, we
can reach out and listen. Where there is frustration and concern, we can offer a place to relax and time to figure things
out.

For today, let's offer "first class" treatment to children.

Doing Things Badly   SEPTEMBER 19

There is an old saying, "A job worth doing is worth doing
right." Doing things right is important for some things – adding numbers correctly, sewing to a pattern as instructed, or
following directions to make cookies.

But the attitude of "doing things right" can also lead to
a sense of perfectionism. "If I can't do it right, I won't do it
at all." Or we feel a need to do it over and over and over
again until we finally get it just right. Perfectionism drains
our energy and robs us of time that could be given to more
positive activities.

Everyone does things badly or makes mistakes along the
way. In fact, this is often the creative environment needed to
inspire a new idea or invention. Making mistakes can lead to
new opportunities we didn't even imagine.

If we always remind children to "be careful," they may
not feel free to explore and take healthy risks to try something different. If we give children a hard time for making a
mistake, this might stifle creativity and encourage limiting
perfectionism.

We all need to be willing to try. Making mistakes is necessary to learn and grow.

Special Needs   SEPTEMBER 20

Like a snowflake, no two children are exactly alike. Every
child has unique needs.

Temperament shapes needs. Some children are very easygoing. Some are cautious and take to changes slowly. Others are active and feisty and respond to life with intensity and drama.

Children also have unique strengths and talents. Some are good readers. Others are great at math. Some are physically coordinated and love active play. Others prefer to play quietly.

Children are influenced by their environment – family, friends, school, teachers. Some children have special needs because of major struggles which have occurred in their family. Others have had difficulty making positive social connections with peers. Still others are born with physical, cognitive, or emotional challenges.

Even though there are some predictable behaviors which arise as children grow, how each child responds is unique. There is no simple formula for development that applies to every child. Getting to know children by careful observation can give us valuable insights.

All children benefit from the support of caring adults who understand their unique needs.

Incentives

We can all be motivated into action when there is the promise of a reward at the end of the task.

> "When I finish with this activity, I am going to
> sit down for a few minutes and relax with a cup
> of tea and a good book."

During a busy week of work, the upcoming weekend lies ahead with time for special projects, play time, and relaxation.

Children also need incentives to motivate them into action.

> "Focus on your homework for 20 minutes
> and then you can take a break and play for 20
> minutes."

> "After we clean up these toys, we'll go for a
> walk."

"When we're finished with this activity, we'll get a game out to play together."

With a little encouragement, children feel inspired to complete the chore and earn the prize.

Short Fuse

When tensions are running high and we are feeling reactive to every little thing, our short fuse can get the best of us and we are likely to explode.

Some people have a feisty personality. They are quick to react. This is true whether they are very happy and excited or very angry. Whether this describes you or your child, there are steps which can be taken to *STOP* the reaction.

*S*low down and *B*reathe
*T*hink before speaking
*E*xplore *O*ptions
*P*ractice *P*atience

We can demonstrate how to deal with our anger and frustrations in healthy ways. We can also be patient as children gradually learn to deal with their feelings appropriately. When we acknowledge a child's feelings, many frustrating situations can be diffused. "I know this is very hard for you. Take a few minutes to calm down, then you will be able to figure out what you need." Our patient response can be soothing to a child.

Bedtime

It comes around at the end of every day when we are *all* tired. Children rarely admit it, but we know we're exhausted! After a busy day, we want to put our feet up and relax. No wonder this is such a challenging time for us all.

Young children have not yet gained an understanding of time. The period between evening and morning can seem like forever. They don't want to miss out on anything. Even though teens realize morning will come, they want to grab all they can from the day and resist sleep, too.

Whether we are talking about toddlers, teens or even adults, a good night's sleep is very important to our health. With a good night's sleep, we can focus better on the task at hand. We have more energy and can think more clearly.

Consistent routines help to prepare children for sleep – quiet activities, a bath or shower, a good book or story time. Children often like to cuddle up and share about their day and plan for tomorrow.

Bedtimes can be difficult. Or they can be a social ritual that offers quality time for quiet interactions.

The Television Trap   SEPTEMBER 24

The television can take on a life of its own. It is so easy to turn on and so hard to turn off. It may even become a central part of our lives. It can rob us of quality time. Instead of playing together, everyone circles around the TV.

When they watch too much, children learn the values they see and hear on television, instead of our own. They don't want to go anywhere or do anything that would keep them from missing their favorite show. Conflicts can also arise between family members when everyone wants to watch their own show.

Television can also be useful. The world opens up. Children can learn things that they would not have the opportunity to see otherwise. But, we need to set reasonable limits so that children are spending more time in play and genuine interaction than absorbed in front of the screen.

TV time is not quality time. Interaction *is* quality time.

The Blame Game   SEPTEMBER 25

"It's not my fault. He made me do it."

Children often want to blame someone else when things go wrong. They kick the table after tripping over it, as if the table leg stuck itself out and made them fall. They want to blame someone else when they forget something – "It's your fault, mom. You didn't remind me to get my homework." They want to blame someone else if they are caught in the act – "It was her idea."

The main rule of the Blame Game is – when there's trouble, whatever happens to me is someone else's fault.

We want children to be able to admit their mistakes and move on to resolve the issue. We help them with this when our reaction to their behavior is reasonable. "I know you didn't mean to spill this, but it needs to be cleaned up. Here's the broom and dustpan." Children can learn to take responsibility for their choices and actions.

Handling Resistance   SEPTEMBER 26

Sometimes, when we ask children to stop what they are doing and do what we need them to do, we meet with resistance, "No, I don't want to!" They have their own ideas about what they want to do. We are more likely to receive a cooperative response if we interrupt gently, give a warning, and allow time to shift gears.

> "I know you are busy right now. I'm letting you
> have ten more minutes with that and then it will
> be time to clean up."

When children resist, and they will, we can calmly respond.

> "I hear you. You don't want to put this away
> right now. But we need to do this before we can
> move on to that."

Sometimes, even when a child is beginning to comply with our request, there are some sound effects. They do not always give up their activity without expressing a little verbal comeback. Try to let this go, as long as positive progress is being made.

When we treat children with respect and patience, we are more likely to receive cooperation.

Let's Compromise

Children see things as black or white.

"You can't do that, you're a girl!"

"This is the way we always play this game!"

"If I can't do it my way, I'm not going to play!"

They can learn to be open to other perspectives. Eventually, we want children to be able to negotiate a reasonable settlement when they are having a disagreement. We want them to realize that cooperation creates winners on both sides. There are reasonable possibilities from both points of view.

So much of life seems to be a competition, with winners and losers. It is no fun to lose. Whether we are talking about siblings, friends, children, or coworkers, a disagreeable atmosphere can lead to bad feelings.

Instead, we can each give a little to find a solution that will work for everyone. We can help children work together.

"She said she is feeling left out. This doesn't seem fair. What are some other things we can do so everyone can play?"

Children can learn to acknowledge each other's feelings and work together to find solutions that work for everyone.

Healthy Boundaries

Where do I stop and you begin? How do I speak up for my own need for personal space? What do I do to encourage each child's independence? Boundaries are the invisible lines that help us define who we are. Boundaries provide personal and emotional protection.

Young children do not realize the importance of boundaries. They climb all over us and each other. They are in your face as they scream for attention. They wrestle in the spirit of fun, until someone gets hurt and it turns into a fight. They do not realize the need to respect other people's things when they pick up something to play with.

We teach about boundaries when we show respect for

other people's privacy by knocking on a door before entering. We teach about boundaries when we honor a child's request to "Stop!" if she is uncomfortable with tickling or wrestling. We teach about boundaries when we ask if a hug would be okay. We teach about boundaries when we ask children to help themselves, even though it might be easier to do it for them.

Ultimately, healthy boundaries are about respect. We respect the other person's right to say "No, I don't like that." or "Yes, I can do that myself."

Hopes and Dreams *September 29*

We have hopes and dreams for children. We hope they will be happy, have good relationships, find a successful career. We hope they will be good people, and will love and be loved. We hope they will learn the necessary social skills. We hope they will follow their own personal dreams *and* demonstrate sensitivity to the needs of others.

When their own hopes closely match the ones we hold for them, we find it easier to accept their path and offer our support. When their dreams diverge from our own expectations, children feel us holding back and resisting. We may even voice our objections. But, our hopes and dreams for them must take a backseat as their own take center stage.

Even though we want the best for them, we cannot fully envision the world in which they will live. Their future is a mystery to us. But we can try to give children the tools they will need to address any challenges they might face. We do this by offering our love and support, providing opportunities, and teaching problem-solving skills. We can offer a supportive environment that helps dreams to come true.

Flexibility in Action *September 30*

Your child comes in the door after school and immediately asks to go to a friend's house. You have established a policy of doing homework right after school to make sure it gets done before it gets too late in the evening.

"No, you can't play with anyone until your homework is done."

Watching your child wiggle and squirm while trying to focus on homework, you realize that there is way too much pent up energy from being in school all day. On second thought, a chance to play and use some of that energy might help him focus better on the homework with less resistance. So, you change your mind –

"I'm sorry. I didn't think first before I answered you. I've changed my mind. It is okay if you go to Eli's house for a while. Just be sure you are back by five o'clock so you can work on your homework before dinner."

Changing our mind is not a weakness. This shows some flexibility. Since even adults make mistakes and sometimes react without thinking, we can apologize and try again. Children learn about flexibility from us. If we are rigid, there is no room for negotiation. Through negotiation, children learn life skills which will help them resolve future conflicts.

October

Safe Passage

There are many twists and turns on the path from childhood to adulthood. It can be a perilous journey. There are dangers and great adventures.

We want safe passage for children. It's our job to protect them as they make their way. We must look out for their physical and emotional well-being. We provide love and acceptance *no matter what*. We reassure them that there is nothing they can ever do or say that will threaten our support for them. We demonstrate our faith in their development. They are growing *just right!* We offer them tools to overcome the obstacles they may face. We teach them communication skills that will help them build effective relationships.

Eventually they must find their own way. But during childhood, we are their providers, their guides, their teachers, their friends. Later, we will step aside as they progress onward into adulthood.

Experience – A Wise Teacher

Nothing provides 100% preparation for parenthood. We learn as we go. The second time around we have experience, but even so, there are still surprises and more lessons to learn.

We would like to save children from the mistakes we have made in the past. We want to offer our experience as a guide. This sometimes works. But much of learning is based on trial and error. Children learn in their own way with their own experiences. They also learn better when they can practice over and over until they finally reach their own "I get it!" moment.

Besides, our life experiences may not be the lessons that children will need for a future we can only imagine. We can offer ideas and suggestions. We can give children rich experiences. But in the end, their own choices and their personal lessons will matter most.

Asking the Right Questions

We become frustrated when children are unwilling to engage in conversation with us.

> "What did you do in school today?"
> "Nothing." Or "Stuff."

It is also easy to stifle communication. We do it all the time by asking Yes/No questions.

> "Do you want to....?" Yes/No
> "Are you.....? Yes/No

We can encourage conversation by asking specific, open-ended questions –

> "What did you play during recess?"
> "What are you working on in your math class?"
> "Did anything funny happen at school today?"
> "You've been frustrated with that game. What seems to be the problem?"

Timing is also important. When children are open to talking, we need to be available. Children often want to share their day if we ask the right questions. After getting their attention by asking a question, it is our turn to focus. The most important component of healthy communication is listening.

The Jealousy Monster

Let's imagine. One day your spouse walks in with a big surprise. Because you love each other so much, your partner brought home another person to live with you and share this love. "We have enough love for everyone." How would you feel about this? Outraged, scared, unappreciated, or maybe even excited ("Good, she can share the chores!").

Is it any wonder that children sometimes have a hard time accepting their brother or sister? Is it really surprising that children fight for our attention? In fact, it's a miracle when there is a smooth adjustment and they interact with very little jealousy.

Siblings have a hard time sharing their parents. They each want to feel special. This doesn't mean that we should always do everything the same way with each child in order to avoid conflict. But we can do our best to love each one in their own special way. We can give attention to each child, even if only for a few minutes.

Sometimes the jealousy is between parents when one of us asks, "How come she *never* does what I ask and responds to you *immediately*?"

No matter where it surfaces, we help to tame the *Jealousy Monster* when we show children that they are each special to us. Even though we are individuals with different needs and abilities, we are all family. We really do have enough love to go around.

No More Tattling   OCTOBER 5

"Mom, he looked at me!"

"Dad, she won't let me play with them!"

Children often tattle because they believe we will protect them. They have learned that we will step in and negotiate this frustrating situation for them. They believe the other child is being unfair, and they want help to set things right. If we step into the middle of a fight between two children, they can turn their anger on us. They are not happy with our solution.

We want children to learn how to solve their own conflicts. Unless someone is being physically hurt or teased, we can stand back, offering assistance only if needed.

"He won't share with me."

"I can tell you are frustrated. But, *you* need to let *him* know how you feel about that. Can you go back there and do that on your own, or would you like me to come with you?"

"I want you to come, too."

"Okay, I will come stand next to you as you
tell him what's bothering you."

It is not comfortable for us to be put in the position of
judge. We can respond to tattling by encouraging communication. Then, stand back. They can work this out.

The "Right Way"   OCTOBER 6

There are many "right ways" to do family life. There is
not one *right* way. But, that is certainly not the impression
we give children. We let them know there is a *right* way to
fold towels. There is a *right* way to do the dishes. There is a
right way to clean the bathroom. We know the best way to
do homework. Some parents even go so far as to discourage
their children from helping with chores because they want it
done the *right* way. So, they do it themselves.

When children reach adulthood, they will do some things
"the way we have always done them." But, they will also
learn to strike out on their own and figure out what is *right*
for them. They will be more prepared for this if they have
had a chance to practice making choices during childhood.

There isn't one *right* way, but there is a wrong way. The
wrong way happens when we forget to encourage children
to make some of their choices and learn what works best for
them.

Weathering Tough Times   OCTOBER 7

Children often have an amazing capacity to cope during
tough times like illness, moving, and other times of family
stress. We need to remember that they are watching and
noticing. When adults are stressed and restless, children feel
it, too.

Children can be helped to understand with simple but
honest explanations that let them know what to expect.
"Mommy is sad because Grandma died. I might be a little
grumpy sometimes. This is not because of you. In fact, I
could use a few extra hugs, okay?"

Routines may be shaken by family stresses. It is important to try to maintain some consistency. Children like to know what is expected of them. We can carve out time in the middle of our busy-ness to give some special one-on-one time to each child.

Children are following our lead, so it is crucial that we take care of ourselves. We need each other even more now. Children often have an incredible capacity for recovery, especially when we are loving, understanding, and patient.

Dealing with Divorce   OCTOBER 8

Divorce touches all of us personally or indirectly. Sometimes, when children hear their parents fighting, they ask, "Are you and daddy getting a divorce?" This may be the furthest thing from your mind, but children have heard about divorce from others. So, any adult fighting can bring up their own fears. Children also need to learn that disagreements do not mean that the next step will be divorce.

If your family does experience a divorce, it is important to reassure children that they did not do anything to bring this on. Since children typically look within to find a cause, we must let them know that this is not their fault.

We can also remind them that both parents still love them. Every effort can be made to try to maintain many of their daily routines. They will be spending time in two households, but their parents will still communicate about kid issues. Parents can continue to follow through with reasonable limits, appropriate routines, and consistency.

Divorce can be hard on children. But we can let them know that they can continue to count on us for love and support.

Imaginary Friends   OCTOBER 9

A four-year-old walks into preschool carrying something tenderly in his hands. When the teacher looks closer, she notices that nothing is there. "Hmm, what do you have there?" The child responds, "This is Jerry. You have to be really quiet. He's asleep."

Some three- or four-year-olds have a very strong relationship with an imaginary friend. This companion does not complain or argue. This friend plays for hours doing whatever the child wants to do. In most cases, imaginary friends are a sign of cleverness and creativity. These children are often able to come up with new ideas and solve problems in situations when others feel frustrated and defeated.

Occasionally, a deep retreat into the imagination may be a result of a traumatic experience. The child may find safety in fantasy, and may feel vulnerable in the real world. In these cases, professional assistance can be helpful. Trained counselors often do "play therapy" that gives the child an opportunity to act out feelings with sand play and toys.

Most often, we are safe in encouraging children to let their imaginations soar. These creative playmates travel with them to fun places.

Evening Routines   October 10

There is so much to do in the evenings: meal preparation, homework, social time, reading, showers, and bed time. And so little energy to do it all. Once children start school, they spend most of their day at school, with friends and away from home. Working and stay-at-home parents are *all* drained by the end of the day.

Even though we are tired, evenings are a precious time to reconnect. We can prepare and eat a meal together. It helps children focus on homework when we are all doing quiet things. We can make ourselves available to hear their stories. We can ask questions to encourage them to share with us.

Having a consistent evening routine helps children know what to expect. We, too, look forward to the calm moments to cuddle up together.

Pull Over!

You are feeling trapped in the car with two angry children. They are fighting with each other about something. The loud noise alone is a hazard to safe driving. You feel your own temper rising, and unless you do something right now, you will lose your cool.

Pull over! Find a safe place to stop the car and get out. Let the kids know that as soon as they stop hassling each other, you will continue on. When we are willing to put up with this momentary inconvenience of pulling over, children learn that their fighting is unacceptable and there is a better way to solve problems. If instead, we yell right back at them, then we are modeling exactly the behavior that we want to stop.

Pulling over works. Not necessarily immediately. And not necessarily after only one time. But, if we are consistent and follow through, next time we can remind them, "If you two can't quiet your voices down, I'm going to pull over and stop. I can't drive safely when you are acting this way." They will listen.

Sometimes we must "pull over" – at the dinner table or in the store or after a frustrating phone call. Pulling over is about taking a personal *time-out*, wherever and whenever needed to regain our calm.

Food Messages

Very young children often know when they are hungry. They stop when they are full. They know what they want and don't want. They have very definite food likes and dislikes.

All too quickly, children get other messages from us about food and eating –

"Oh, you can't be hungry now."

(But she is!)

"This is yummy and good for you."

(It doesn't taste good to the child.)

"I don't want you to leave the table until you've finished your carrots and turkey."

(He is full and wants to get up to play.)

"I'm sorry you're disappointed. Have a cookie."

(What does this have to do with it?)

Children learn to ignore their own body and its hunger or satisfaction signals. They learn to eat when they are not hungry. They learn to eat when they are bored or excited or disappointed. They learn to eat more, even when they are already full.

We can help children learn healthy eating habits. We can offer healthy foods and encourage them to listen to their body and eat moderately when they are feeling hungry.

Sticks and Stones OCTOBER 13

"Sticks and stones can break my bones,
but words can never hurt me."

This childhood proverb has good intentions. Adults want to let children know that they have a choice and can let hurtful words roll off their backs. But, words do hurt. In fact, the scars of these long ago experiences often remain well into adulthood.

We can arm children with communication tools to deflect these cutting comments –

"I don't like it when you say those things to me.
It hurts. I am not going to stay here and play if
you can't use nicer words."

We can also consider our own communication. Sometimes we say things in a "bark" and with a "bite." Instead of snarling,

"What are you doing? How many times do I
have to remind you..."

We can explain in a calm, but firm voice –

"Please stop that now. That is dangerous. Come
over here and do this instead."

What we say and how we say it does matter. Words can hurt. Or words can help build relationships.

"What, Me Worry?" OCTOBER 14

You bet! We worry! We want the best for children. We feel their pain and frustration –

> When things don't go as expected.
> When he is late.
> When she is not doing well in school.
> When he is struggling to learn something new.

We imagine the worst! "Oh, my! What if...?"

Take a deep breath! Relax! What good is our worrying, anyway? We want children to consider the possible consequences of their behavior. We want them to think about what they want and what they need to learn to get there.

Thinking positively is much more likely to lead to rewarding results. Our encouraging support is usually welcome and much more likely to be helpful. Worry drains us. Hopeful positive thoughts energize us and open up the doors of possibility for children.

Seeing the Strengths OCTOBER 15

> "I'm just so worn out. Everything is a fight with him. He is so sensitive and expects all of us to jump to his demands."

Sound familiar? We can label this child as feisty, demanding, dramatic, and overly sensitive. *Or,* we can look at this behavior a different way, seeing the strengths. He is determined, independent, quick, and creative.

Very often, finding a solution to any issue involves discovering the strengths. In the heat of the moment, try to give yourself time to think. Be careful to avoid matching your child's high-strung energy with your own.

Acknowledge feelings. "I know you are feeling frustrated right now, but we have other commitments and can not do what you would like. Maybe later." Then, we disengage and let the tensions ease. "I hear you. This isn't what you expected. I'm going into the other room to finish folding the clothes. You can join me when you are ready to talk about what we might do next."

Once the stresses of the moment are soothed, he is much more likely to use his inner strengths and creativity to find a mutually agreeable solution.

Kiddle in the Middle   OCTOBER 16

It's so hard to feel stuck in the middle. The oldest child will always have a special place. Parents practice and learn from the oldest child. But, everything is also new and surprising. Parents become devoted to their firstborn, as they fall madly in love with that amazing creature, and with their new role as a parent.

When the next baby comes along, the first is still making demands. Yet, with two parents and two sets of arms, there is room for everyone's needs. If the second child remains the youngest and the baby, there is a chance for a reasonable time share between parents. But, if a third child comes along, many of the needs of the second child must wait. The firstborn is considered old enough to be independent. So, whether ready or not, the middle child waits, too, because the newest baby needs attention.

Birth order is important, but it need not be a major issue. We can help each child feel special. They each have unique gifts and talents. They can each be charming in their own way. They can each be helpful. They are each creative. We can make time for tender moments with each child!

Supporting Learning   OCTOBER 17

Children do better in school when parents are involved in their education. Parents have valuable information to share with teachers about their child's unique learning style. They know their strengths and understand their interests.

Parents can support their child's education in some important ways.

> *Read to them* – The world opens up to a child who knows how to read.

> *Answer their questions* – Children are naturally curious. Curiosity is a very important part of learning. *Listen* to them and give them a chance to ask questions. Respond simply and honestly.

> *Homework time* – Create a quiet place for doing homework. It also helps when *everyone* in the family is doing quiet activities at the same time so the child is not distracted by someone else's *fun*.

> *Volunteer in the classroom* – Go in every few months to offer your assistance.

> *Our education* – If you have not finished your own education or have interest in learning new things, do so. Children are very proud of us when we go to classes.

We show children the value of education by supporting theirs.

Be Yourself   October 18

We want children to feel comfortable enough to be themselves. This can be difficult in the face of peer pressure to be like the rest of the crowd. Each group has its own signature – clothes, hair, talk, interests. Some things are "cool." And if you are not, you are *not*!

We want children to be able to stand up for what is important to them. We want them to be able to resist going along with the crowd, especially when the activity or attitude might be an unhealthy choice. We want them to be able to say, "Hey, if you're going to do that, I'm out of here!"

In order to stand up for themselves, they need to practice. Who better to practice on than us? We help them practice their independence when we give them choices. It is also important to accept their anger or resistance to our requests, and not take it personally. Sometimes we can be flexible and back off. We can remember that they are learning to be assertive and stand up to pressure from others.

Forgiveness   OCTOBER 19

Someone has said or done something hurtful. Children yell at each other and fight over toys, activities, or being first. Teens are angry at us for enforcing a restriction that just "isn't fair." We also carry resentments because of hurts inflicted by spouse, co-workers, children, or neighbors. No one is immune. We all get our feelings hurt.

Young children usually forget quickly. One minute they can be very angry at us for imposing a limit and the next minute they are happily climbing into our arms. Teens have longer memories.

When we can not forgive, we carry resentments and bitterness which continue to injure us and hurt our relationships. At some point, it is time to forgive and move on. We are not excusing the behavior. We are distinguishing the behaviors and choices from the person's character. In most cases, the other person did not intend the hurt. When we forgive, we are pardoning the person whose behavior hurt us.

Forgiveness involves communication, "It really hurt my feelings when you said that. I know you didn't mean to upset me, but it did." Now, we can let it go and move on.

The Boy Who Cried "Wolf!"   OCTOBER 20

Most of us were told this story as children. A boy thought he would tease the townspeople and so twice he cried "Wolf!" Each time they came running, concerned that he needed some help protecting the sheep. He got a big laugh out of their panic. Then he really saw the wolf, and shouted sincerely, "Wolf!" The people heard him, thought he was teasing them again, and decided not to respond. This time the wolf was a reality and the consequences were very unfortunate.

Children tell stories. Their stories can be innocent or they can be hurtful. Sometimes children don't like the way things really are, so what they say is wishful thinking, "I finished all my homework at school."

Sometimes children are afraid of the consequences of their behavior. They are afraid of our reaction to the truth. So, they tell a story. "I didn't break that. I don't know how it happened."

When we know what really happened, we need not ask, "Why did you do that?" or "What's going on here?" Instead, we can make a statement, "Hmm, the milk spilled. Let's get a sponge and clean it up." This way, there is no need to hide.

Children are more likely to be honest when they know our response will be reasonable and patient. When we are approachable adults, they are much more likely to feel safe enough to speak the truth.

What's for Dessert? OCTOBER 21

This is not what you're expecting: suggestions on the most nutritious desserts for children or remedies for finicky eaters. This is about looking for and discovering the "sweetness" in our life with children.

At any given moment we can usually describe at least three of our current challenges or frustrations with family life. How often do we take the time to recognize the sweet things about each child?

> The dimple on the left side when he smiles;
> Her willingness to help;
> That sneaky grin when she knows she is not
> supposed to be doing this;
> That voice so full of excitement when describing his latest treasure;
> The peacefulness of sleep;
> The way her whole body gets into it as she
> dances to the music;

The tentative hug that only a teen boy can give.
We have many sweet experiences with children.

Entitlement OCTOBER 22

Sometimes children give the impression that they expect to be allowed to do whatever they want, whenever they want. Or a child might become resentful when we don't have the "right" bread for a sandwich. They feel entitled.

Children are entitled to our love and understanding. They need adults in their lives who pay attention to their basic needs. They are entitled to be listened to when they are feeling frustrated or excited.

But there are also many times when they will be disappointed. We remind them that certain things are not to be taken for granted. When they express a sense of entitlement, we can respond in various ways –

"I know we did that once, but that does not
mean it's a guarantee every time."
"I'm sorry, we don't have time to do that
today."
"I know you would like me to do that for
you, but I am confident you can do that for
yourself."

We want children to grow up with a commitment to cooperation.

Stinkin' Thinkin' OCTOBER 23

"I can't..." "You never..." "I'm ugly..." "I hate you!"

We appreciate it when children are kind and respectful. We would really like them to develop self-worth. We hope they will feel capable. We want them to feel confident to try new things. We also hope they feel loved and accepted as they are.

But, some days don't go well and negativity rises to the surface. Just like us, children sometimes become critical of others, or shout negative "self-talk." These frustrations are real. Sometimes our own hurtful words said about others, or ourselves, have influenced the children around us.

Children want us to hear what is underneath the words. What do these words say about how they are feeling? What does he really need right now?

One of the most powerful needs we all have is to be heard. We can acknowledge the feelings behind the words. Our response to "I can't do this" can be "I can tell you are really upset" rather than "Don't be silly, of course you can!" This alone can diffuse the situation and open the doors of communication so that we can talk about what is really wrong.

We can look beyond the "stinkin' thinkin'" to see what is really troubling this child.

Self Doubt   OCTOBER 24

When did this sweet, capable child start to doubt her worth or value? Or question his ability?

Until they learn otherwise, many children believe they can do anything. Certainly, they try and they experiment. Some children find this easier than others. They take risks and push themselves and us to the limits. Others are more cautious. But, over time, messages get planted in their heads –

"You can't!"

"You're too little."

"Why do you want to do that?"

Eventually this internal self-talk can become a wall that prevents children from trying new things. They lose confidence and doubt their ability to succeed. We understand this, because we experience self-doubt, too.

Encouragement can conquer doubts. "Hang in there! You can do it!" Affirmations help to quiet these negative messages.

Release Me

Sometimes we are exhausted. We don't want to be a mother, a father, or a teacher any more. We don't want to worry. We don't want to stand by, feeling helpless. We even imagine what it might be like to live in a fairy tale world where dreams come true and everyone lives "happily ever after."

But this isn't a fairy tale! This is real life, where things are messy. We can't just snap our fingers and make everything okay. People say, "Just let it go," as if it's easy to just open our clutching hands and release our grip. But, it's *not* that easy. We have to work at doing the best we can every day.

We look forward to the time when our children will have their own grown-up lives. And deep inside, we really do believe that they have what they need to make a good life.

Power

We don't have the power to change our children, our boss, our partner, or our neighbor. We do have the power to change ourselves – what we believe, how we feel, what we can do or accomplish, how we react to others, and what we will or will not accept.

When we change ourselves, those around us often follow along in response. The old patterns of interaction no longer work for them either.

So when we are going through a period of change, we can realize that everyone is affected. We are in this together. We can all learn new ways of communicating, expressing our feelings, and playing together.

Sometimes we feel so powerless. What can we possibly do to help ourselves and our children make healthy changes in order to grow? We do have power. We have the power of calm responses, acceptance, unconditional love, and effective communication, right here and right now.

We can use our power to respond to children with love, respect, and kindness.

Learning to Give

Children can be so generous. When we are not feeling well, a toddler will share her blanket. When a friend's feelings are hurt, a child will try to comfort him. Many children seem to have a natural gift of generosity. But, our consumer-oriented times can quickly turn the focus from giving to receiving. It is up to us to keep the spirit of kindness, giving, and cooperation alive.

> We can give our time to volunteer at a school
> or the public library.
> We can donate well-loved toys to service
> projects.
> We can pass on our still-wearable clothes to
> others in need.

Children learn about generosity from our good examples. When we give, so much comes back to us.

Homework Hassles

It is inevitable! Children will be given homework and they will not always be willing to sit down and do it without coaching. After spending at least six hours at school, sitting down to do more is often the farthest thing from their minds. We can not totally prevent children's frustrations with school expectations. But we can create a supportive environment which helps them focus on homework.

Know your child. Timing is important. Does your child need some time after school to wind down, relax, and play? Or does your child relax more easily when homework is completed?

Provide a comfortable, well-lit space to improve concentration. If everyone in the household is doing paperwork or reading, this lowers the distractions. It helps when the TV is off and all are engaged in quiet activities. We can also break the study time into manageable blocks. It is sometimes hard to focus without breaks.

Encourage children to keep a calendar of due dates. Then we can plan ahead and know when there is time for special activities or when they must be postponed.

We can create a supportive study environment which eases some of the hassles.

The Fear's for Real   OCTOBER 29

Children's fears are very real, even if we know they are not based in reality. If a child is afraid of a monster under the bed or in the closet, that "monster" is real. Children feel empowered when we dramatically sweep under the bed or close the closet door.

When children are afraid of the dark, we can reassure them that we are nearby. We can also provide a flashlight or a nightlight to illuminate the darkness.

If the fear is about spiders or bugs, it is cruel to tease by dangling the creature in the child's face. Knowledge can ease fears, so books can help a child understand this creature. We can also put it in a jar where it can be safely watched.

Children are sometimes afraid of abandonment. It is important that we say good-bye before leaving them with a sitter. Clocks can help, "I will be back by eight o'clock." Our timely return reminds them that we can be trusted.

We can let them know that everyone is afraid sometimes. Children learn to overcome their fears with positive experiences. Once they gain confidence, they can stand up to some scary things.

Falling in Love Again   OCTOBER 30

How did you feel when you first met your child? Was there an infant in the entire world that could have been more beautiful or more precious? Or maybe your love for your child grew more gradually. Maybe you didn't feel that intense love immediately. But, at some point, you realized you would do anything to protect this child!

Then the toddler years came, and this angel began to

resist and assert her will, "No!" Tantrums flared. Where is my sweet child? Your school-aged child has his mind set on what he wants right now. Your teen doesn't want to have anything to do with you or the entire family.

Loving children can be an ongoing challenge. There are times when it is not easy. But, we can get beyond the hard times and this disagreeable attitude to see the child we love.

Your precious child is still there. Hear her laugh. See his smile. Share the excitement of a new accomplishment. Feel that warm hug. Noticing and remembering helps us to fall in love, again and again!

Sweet Dreams, Dear One   OCTOBER 31

So many possibilities. What are your dreams for your child?

love	comfort
adventure	companions
challenges	joys and pleasure
safety	strength and endurance

We all have dreams and hopes for children. We can use our dreams for them to gauge our own behavior and expectations. We can remember to consider what we are doing to help them become all that they can be. We can offer the love and support that opens the doors of opportunity and offers assistance along the way.

We have dreams for children. But, in the end, it is up to each of us to follow our own dreams. What children become is really up to them. We offer our love, support, and our blessings.

Sweet dreams, dear one.

November

Learning Styles

Children learn in different ways. Some are good at math, while others are great readers. Some like working in groups, while others prefer to work alone. Some have a talent for art or music, while still others prefer sports and actively use their bodies in everything they do. Children feel comfortable with their individual talents and often feel uneasy when required to do things that do not come easily.

The typical classroom is not always set up to encourage all the learning styles. Schools focus primarily on math, reading, and the sciences. Some children may feel left out or frustrated with these school expectations.

There are many different paths to learning and reaching one's potential. Adults are important advocates for children. We recognize their strengths. We understand how they learn. A strong partnership between parents and teachers helps children succeed.

The following seven days will illustrate different learning styles. As their advocates, we help children find a learning environment which best supports their individual needs.

Bookworm

He always has his head in a book. His library card is maxed out and he has his favorite authors on hold.

Words are very important to her. She loves storytelling. She enjoys word games. Her diary is her special friend where she writes about all of her secrets and dreams. In school, she does well in most of the subjects that require reading and writing.

This child is sometimes challenged by the need to leave the books long enough to interact with friends. He prefers working alone. He may not enjoy outdoor activities, so he loves rainy days when he has a built-in excuse to curl up with a good book.

Since she is comfortable with words, she is a great debater. We can also use her word strength to reason with

her when a rule needs to be reinforced or an explanation given. Words can be the key that opens the doors to a wide world of possibilities.

Math Wizard NOVEMBER 3

Numbers are always running through his head. He sees relationships between addresses. He calculates the totals in the grocery store and counts the stars in the sky. Car license plates create a math challenge. Math and science are the obvious favorite school subjects.

In addition to a fascination with numbers, she loves logic puzzles. She also has an answer for everything. Her thoughts are well formed and she believes that she's right!

Since these children do well with math, other children envy this talent. So, they may experience teasing and social isolation. Even one friend with similar interests can make all the difference.

Everyone has gifts and talents. Children need adults who will help them strike a balance in their interests and activities. Children also need friends and family members who will help them learn cooperative social skills.

The Budding Artist NOVEMBER 4

Words and phrases that might describe this child include:

creative	impractical
inventive	day dreamer
imaginative	head in the clouds
visionary	unfocused

But give her a pen or paints or other creative media and she dreams up something amazing. Her doodles are pure art which actually help her focus on conversations, rather than distracting her. Sometimes her ideas seem quirky or odd, but often they include a workable seed of possibility. She has an accurate visual memory.

This child sees things differently than most. Aware of his

physical environment, he notices colors, facial expressions, and visual relationships between objects. He learns best in a flexible environment which encourages creativity and allows for the unexpected.

Creative...Inventive...Visionary. With the doors of imagination open, who knows what the future holds? The unique gifts of each child are needed to solve the world's problems and make this a place where we all can thrive.

Nature Lover   NOVEMBER 5

He can often be found playing in the dirt. His pockets are full of stones, feathers, and sticks. He loves creeks or water of any kind. He finds bugs, worms, and every crawly, squirmy, or flying creature. He knows their names and can explain their biological processes.

She notices details. She sees things. Not just in nature but anytime. If you move something in the living room, she sees it. If you change your shirt in the middle of the day, she notices.

He wears out shoes and the knees of his pants because he is busy exploring. He doesn't mind being dirty, and needs a bath *every* day.

This child loves everything about nature and is happiest outside, sun or rain. So, the restraints of school just might be too much. Reading is fun if it involves insect identification. Math is okay when it involves counting the number of ants carrying eggs into an ant hole. Art time is an opportunity to draw something found under a rock. We can advocate for the nature lover, by encouraging teachers to include activities which appeal to this child's interests.

Through children's eyes, we can experience the pure excitement and joy of discovery that the latest natural treasure brings. Enjoy this child!! There is a place in this world for every child.

Social Butterfly

She needs contact and interaction. She is happiest when she is right in the thick of it all. She bosses others around but she can also take leadership pretty seriously.

When there is no one around to play with, he feels lost. He will call all of his friends in search of someone to hang out with. And if he finds no one, watch out! He may follow you around talking your ear off or demanding that you play a game with him.

She prefers to work in groups. She enjoys studying with others. She likes the social interactions involved in a group project with planning and brainstorming, generating ideas and working things out. She also has a nurturing side and is very concerned when someone does not feel included.

He is challenged by situations that call for quiet solo work. He gets into trouble for disturbing those next to him who are trying to work independently. He interrupts others often and may find it hard to wait his turn. He likes being the center of attention.

These children have a gift for leadership and will probably develop strong people skills. Though their social energy can sometimes feel exhausting, these children have many strengths.

Music to My Ears

Toe tapping
Fingers dancing on the tabletop
Humming a tune in the hallway

This child has natural musical talent. He has a passion for singing, playing an instrument, or drumming a rhythm whenever and wherever. If this child is feeling sad or frustrated, his mood is lifted by music. This child may actually study better, with greater attention and focus, when music is playing. Soft music might help her to fall asleep at night. She notices sounds in the environment and will tell you if you left the water running.

These creative expressions are equally as valuable as a technical understanding of numbers or the power of words. Our abilities and gifts are doorways into who we are, what we value, and where we will go in life.

Experts realize that the creative arts are worthy sources for learning self-discipline, focus and responsibility. Children who are encouraged to follow a musical path of self-expression often gain skills in other areas. Their pleasure and creativity is "music to our ears."

Marching to a Different Drummer   NOVEMBER 8

Some children seem to march to their own drummer from day one. These children are very independent. They are sometimes described as "self-starters" because they have their own way of doing things and are not easily influenced. These children often prefer to work alone. Since being a "team player" is usually highly prized, the child who does not want to go along with the group activity may feel unappreciated.

There is room in this world for many different kinds of people. Some jobs actually require more independence. In fact, significant new innovations have often been invented by people willing to look at things in unexpected ways.

A child who marches to his or her own internal motivations may regularly come into conflict with peers, parents, and other adults. This child needs to learn to be respectful of others at the same time as she stands up for her own needs.

"I really don't want to, but thanks for asking."

An adult's love and understanding may help this child navigate the social landscape. We can learn to accept and support each child's unique style.

In Need of Distraction   NOVEMBER 9

We can imagine any number of activities or behaviors that get children in trouble with us. They are getting into something that is not theirs. They are tempting the fates and doing something potentially dangerous. They are avoiding our attempt to remind them of the rules and doing the unacceptable anyway. It feels like they are ignoring us.

An effective discipline response that gets too little credit is distraction. Children are very focused on whatever they are doing right now. They are not doing this to get in trouble with us. Children are curious explorers. For example, young children see us using our phones all the time. They don't understand why it is off limits for them. We need to explain simply and then distract their interest by giving a substitute toy or suggesting an activity which will redirect attention away from the phone.

It is not enough to just say "No!" no matter how loud. Our active redirection is more likely to successfully stop the inappropriate behavior. "That's dangerous. Come here and do this instead." Or, "We can't do that right now. We *can* do this."

Children need a little help from us to learn what we expect. They are in need of some distraction to refocus their curiosity to safe, acceptable activities.

Body Language NOVEMBER 10

Did you realize that more than 70% of our communication is non-verbal? Gestures, eye contact, tone of voice, and shoulder slump are all body language.

Watch children from a distance. What do they tell us about how they are feeling? As they move into the school-aged years and then into adolescence, it is important to read the body clues that tell us where this conversation might be going or how each child is feeling. Maybe their body language is saying that the child is frustrated, overwhelmed, afraid, concerned, excited, discouraged, or pleased. We can respond by saying,

> "I can see that I've been talking too much and you're tired of this. We can talk about this later."

Children also notice our body language. Our words don't always reflect what we are really feeling, and children can see this. We need to be clear and honest with both. It helps to ask ourselves, "What might my body be saying to my child about how I am really feeling?"

Our communication is most effective when our words and our body are relaying the same message.

"He Made Me Do It!"   NOVEMBER 11

Passing the buck. What child hasn't tried to duck responsibility by blaming someone else? One of our tasks is to help children understand the importance of accepting responsibility for their behavior. We want them to realize that no one can really make them do anything. Children need to learn that they always have choices. They can choose how they will respond in any situation.

> "I know he asked you and you felt obligated to
> do that with him. But you didn't have to. You
> made a choice. You can also choose to say 'no'
> and do something else."

The same thing is true for us. Children don't make us yell at them. We sometimes react before thinking. Children don't give us this headache. We are stressed out and avoiding healthier alternatives. Children don't drive us crazy. We are forgetting to do the self-care needed to keep our patience up and our frustrations at bay.

We all have choices. We can choose how we will react. We can choose what we will say. We can choose whether to yell or take a time-out. We can choose to be overwhelmed or make time for self-care.

Difficult Child?   NOVEMBER 12

Let's set things straight. There are no difficult children. There are children who have behaviors that are challenging. But, the same child can also be charming and thoughtful.

Our goal is to help children to experience success. We want children to be all they can be.

Negative labels do not help children. We don't want them to call each other hurtful names. It is also not helpful for children to be identified as a "brat" or a "troublemaker." When they hear this often, they may begin to believe it themselves and act out with behaviors which justify the label.

Instead, we can separate the child from the behavior. Children need to learn that their behavior is often a choice. They can choose to be kind and cooperative, or not. They can choose to get their work done, or not. Sometimes, the choice is more elusive. When anyone is tired or frustrated, it can show in behavior.

Regardless of their current behavior, all children are good kids. They each start out with the potential for greatness.

Silencing the Critic   NOVEMBER 13

We all have voices in our heads that are talking to us all the time. And we need to encourage this inner cheerleader –

"You go, girl!!"
"You can do it!"
"Go for it."

Often the loudest voice is our "inner critic."

"That was stupid!"
"You're never going to finish that!"
"What made you think you could do that?"

There is nothing positive to be said about this hurtful voice. We feel discouraged, powerless, and incapable. Even though we may have heard these voices in the past, we can avoid passing on similar messages to children.

When the critical judge speaks, we can counter with a protective, encouraging voice. We can say,

"I realize this seems difficult, but you can do it,
one foot in front of the other. Give it a try!"

Or for yourself as you tell the critic to "Stop!" –

"I need to be patient with myself. This is new for me, but I have the skills I need to accomplish this!"

We can give children *and ourselves* honest and encouraging feedback. We can accomplish many things when we believe in ourselves!

Too Busy Lives   NOVEMBER 14

Our lives sometimes feel like they are spinning out of control. Days start early as we rise and get children ready for child care or school. Dressed and fed, the car is loaded and children are delivered to their caregivers. After a sometimes weepy, difficult good-bye, mothers and fathers are off to their own busy days – either at home or in the work world.

Non-stop responsibilities continue. Children go from child care to school then to after-school care before being picked up late in the afternoon. Sometimes children have music lessons and sports events before going home. Evening routines are full with meal preparation, dinner, chores, homework, and bedtime.

Even though life is full, we can make the in-between times pleasurable. As we go through our daily routines, we can talk and laugh with our children. We can share stories from our day. We can slow down, too.

Children grow up so quickly. When our lives are too busy, we miss many wonderful opportunities to enjoy their childhood.

Doing What I Say   NOVEMBER 15

Children learn from our behavior. When we follow through and do what we say, children learn to trust us. The relationship between adults and children is enhanced when they can count on us.

"In ten minutes we'll start getting ready for bed." (You set a timer – and you do)

"As soon as this chore is finished, we will go to
      the park." (And you do)

Doing what we have said requires that we think before speaking. In the midst of a conflict, we sometimes react quickly. We may need to respond immediately if someone is getting hurt. At other times, we are stressed or hurried and just forget to think.

Following through is important, but sometimes we regret what we have said. If that happens, we can admit our mistake and try again, with a more appropriate response. Thinking first helps prevent mistakes.

We can slow down and think carefully before responding. When we do what we say, children are learning to trust us.

Making a Comeback

Recovering from a setback can feel overwhelming. We are very frustrated and disappointed when things don't go as we expected. It can be hard to get back up after we stumble. There's no avoiding setbacks. Bad things happen – a long illness, a poor grade after intense studying, changing schools mid-year, a difficult divorce, the loss of a good friend.

Though we can't control the comings and goings of these life challenges, we can choose what kind of attitude we will adopt to deal with them. We can complain OR we can stand up, dust ourselves off, accept this, and face the music.

With a little support and encouragement, we can try again.

"Come on, I know this is hard right now. But, I
      believe in you and I'm right here beside you."

Setbacks happen. Where we go next is really up to us. The children are watching. We can teach them the coping skills to handle setbacks and the survival skills to move on. We can learn to make successful comebacks after hard times.

The *Guilt Monster* is always lurking around the corner or sitting on our shoulder. We love our kids and want the best for them. But, parent guilt is probably inevitable. No matter how hard we try, we make mistakes. We sometimes feel like we have ruined our child's chances for a healthy adulthood.

Our rational side knows this is not true. We really don't have that much power to control anyone (sometimes not even ourselves). But, our vulnerable side believes we have blown it! Actually, a little healthy guilt helps us think about what we did, learn from it, and then change.

There are things we can do to keep the *Guilt Monster* at bay –

> We can *be realistic*. No one is perfect. And children love us even when we make mistakes.

> We can do our best to *take care of ourselves* – eat right, get enough sleep, exercise daily, listen to music, and have fun.

> It helps to *connect with others*. We are not alone. Everyone gets the "guilty blues."

> Finally, positive self-talk helps. We need to stop taking ourselves so seriously, *work on our attitude, and lighten up*.

The *Guilt Monster* probably won't go away. But we can put him in his place...in the background.

Independence to Interdependence   NOVEMBER 18

Many of us were raised to be independent. We were encouraged to be an individual and think for ourselves. We demonstrated self-reliance when we completed a task on our own. We were asked to make our own choices and decisions. We learned to do things without help from others.

Others were raised with an emphasis on family responsibilities. It was important that our behavior reflected well on the family. We were encouraged to be helpful. There were few personal choices. The family's way was the "right" way.

We need each other. With interdependence, we have each other's needs and interests at heart when we make decisions. We can respect each other's talents and encourage individual expression. Together we can accomplish many things.

There are times when independence is called for and times when interdependence is appropriate. Children need to learn to take care of themselves by dressing on their own or completing their homework. They also need to realize that at other times life goes more smoothly when everyone offers help and works together.

Holiday Planning   NOVEMBER 19

The holidays can be wonderful times. We gather to visit with family and friends. We share good food and fun times.

Holidays can also be very stressful. Lots of effort goes into the planning and preparations to try to meet everyone's expectations. We may feel pressured to follow traditions which are not our own. Even in the best of times, it may feel like too much – too much busy-ness, too much interaction, too much food, too much go-go-go!

Remember, holidays are for everyone. When possible, include children in the planning. Ask them what they would like to do. Break up sit-and-talk times with active play times. Make sure to plan for plenty of fun.

Though our routines typically change during the holidays, children get grumpy if they are over-tired or overwhelmed. When planning holiday events, remember to schedule a balance of activities so that there are opportunities for fun *and* time to relax.

Like a Guest   NOVEMBER 20

"Treat your children like guests in your home."

This is a bold statement. But what it means is – children deserve the same respect and acceptance that we would give to visitors in our home. If your guest spills his drink during dinner, you wouldn't think of giving him a hard time,

> "How many times have I told you not to play with your food! If you would just sit still, this wouldn't happen!"

Of course we would not say this to a guest! We might say, "It's okay. It will clean up quickly with this towel." We can treat children with the same respect. That spilled milk was not an intentional act. It was an accident.

We help children learn when we offer loving guidance. They deserve our respect during all of our interactions.

Giving Thanks NOVEMBER 21

This is the season to acknowledge our gratitude. Many of us will gather with family and friends, and spend hours preparing a meal that will be all finished in a few minutes. Some folks crowd around the television and watch parades and football games. Children fight for our attention.

The real meaning of the holidays is not about eating way more food in one day than we need in an entire week! The "thanks-giving" holiday is a time to remember that we have many things for which we are grateful.

> Loving and supportive family members
> Good friends
> Our health
> A warm, comfortable home
> Time to socialize and play together
> Good books and the ability to read them
> Fun games to play together
> Helpful teachers

We can give thanks for the many relationships and experiences that give us comfort and joy.

Home Sweet Home

What goes into creating *Home Sweet Home*? *Home* is not about the house or dwelling, the physical structure of a residence. *Home* is about the neighborhood and community. But more importantly, *Home* is about the people who live inside and their relationships.

> Home is a place where everyone feels welcome.
> Home is cozy and comfortable.
> Home is warm and friendly.
> Home is full of love.
> Home is safe.
> Home is a place where people communicate.
> Home is a place where neighborhood kids gather.

Working together, we make a house into a home.

Home is where the heart is.

Taking the Bait

Your child says or does something to grab your attention. It may be disrespectful or just plain annoying. Buttons are pushed and we react. When a child says something like, "I'm bored!" or "You never let me....", we often want to take the bait and offer our own comeback:

> "Now stop that. You know that's not true. You don't appreciate what I do."

Don't take the bait. Stay calm. Instead, acknowledge this child's feelings:

> "I can tell you're frustrated. What do you need?"

We can learn how to respond to children in healthy ways. They also learn from our positive comments. Clear communication is more likely to get them the attention they really want.

Going Ballistic NOVEMBER 24

Sometimes a day has gone so well that you decide to reward your child with a few extra stay-up minutes. You want to acknowledge your child's efforts today. But, as bedtime approaches, you realize its too much and your child loses it.

Timing is everything. At the end of a very busy day, even if everything has gone really well, sometimes children have no more reserves left and experience a meltdown. She spent an enormous amount of energy during the day maintaining her cool. Now that she is home and in her comfort zone, she feels safe enough to let go and release all her feelings.

We need to remember not to go ballistic ourselves. Breathe. She's not doing this to get to you. She needs hugs and support, and probably a good night's sleep. When we realize we overreacted and got angry, a hug helps us, too.

Everyone becomes overwhelmed sometimes. Rest and healthy habits help us maintain our cool.

Admitting Our Mistakes NOVEMBER 25

Do you ever beat yourself up thinking you've really blown it today? You yelled. You were way too harsh when the situation really didn't warrant it. You were inflexible and wanted it done your way. Understandably, children respond to us with anger, sadness, disappointment, or a sense of powerlessness.

We all have bad days, days when we overreact, when we are not patient. At these times, apologizing is a sign of strength, not weakness. Children learn from our example. We are saying, "I made a mistake. I shouldn't have yelled." Once we apologize, we can still take a firm stand on the issue with love and respect.

Thankfully, children are willing to forgive. They realize we are not perfect. Everyone makes mistakes. When we have mended the hurt, and set the necessary limit, there is still time to start fresh. We can heal the hurts and move on with love.

The Blessings of Friends

To have friends, we must learn to be a friend. And when we have friends, there are many rewards.

Children learn about friends from an early age. Initially, they watch and play alongside each other. As their imagination grows, they interact more with each other. Eventually, their friendships become deeper. Some of us still have friends from childhood.

Children learn about friendship from us. We can model healthy friendships. Children realize through observing us that friends offer: fun, laughter and good times, shared experiences, unconditional love and acceptance, and support during hard times, or anytime!

I Believe

What are the beliefs that guide your steps? What beliefs influence your daily choices and decisions? Does your life really reflect what is most important to you? Or are other messages expressed through your lifestyle?

"Hurry up!"

"Be quiet! I'm watching this TV show."

"Do it my way, now!"

"Me first!"

We can send positive messages in our words and our actions that reflect our most valued priorities –

Children are amazing individuals.

Family is important.

Play and relaxation are daily essentials.

Everyone has a say in our decisions.

Kindness and cooperation are valued.

We are all part of a much larger world family. The beliefs that guide us start in our home. Children do what we do and say what we say. They are watching and listening.

Bringing Along Our Baggage

Whether we like it or not, we all carry baggage from our childhoods. For some of us, this is like a very heavily loaded backpack. This baggage includes all of the messages we received and the experiences we gathered from family, friends, and our cultural community –

Expectations and "shoulds"
Value judgments and "Not good enoughs"
Memories – happy and sad
Role models – positive, negative, and absent
Experiences that supported who we were
Frustrations and disappointments

We learned many things during our childhoods that are useful for us today. Some of our past experiences may not be as helpful. In spite of it all, we can choose how much we will let past experiences influence us today. We can decide *right now* to create a positive life for ourselves and our children.

Time Flies

When we are in the middle of the demands of a busy day, it seems the day will never end! But, more often time flies by far too quickly. There are so many things to do and so little time to do them all. Too soon we turn around and our baby has become a toddler, a child, a teen. He has reached another milestone. She's all grown up!

We can't stop time. But when we are more present to each moment, we experience a richer life. The past is gone. The future looms ahead, but life and joys, discoveries and challenges are all here now.

Notice the miraculous growth and learning
Cherish the questions
Savor the sweet hugs and kisses
Enjoy the unquenchable curiosity
Appreciate the unstoppable energy
Treasure the bonds of family

Too soon, children are grown. How much better for us all when we are intentional about making memories today, right now! Yes, time flies, but we can enjoy the moments we have.

Doing Our Best   NOVEMBER 30

Raising children is one of the most challenging jobs we will ever have. Children depend upon us to provide a healthy environment, offer love, and give support at all the right times. Even with all of the stress this brings, we manage to do it. One day at a time.

Looking back, we have days that have gone well. Sure, we have had some hassles getting out of the house in the morning. Or we have struggled with our child over homework or the nighttime routines. But as we tuck them in at night, we realize that we made it through another day.

There are days or weeks that are overwhelming. On top of our typically busy days, extra crises arise. There are problems with family finances, school struggles, endless sibling fights, or illness on top of illness.

In spite of it all, our hearts are in the right place. We have paid attention to them. We have answered their questions. We have fed them and chauffeured them. We have read to them and encouraged their independence. We have held them and listened to them. We have done our best.

We deserve our best, too. Self-care helps us sustain our energies. All we can reasonably do IS the best we can do.

December

Living Our Values

Children learn from the many daily examples they see. Sometimes they are *our* teachers! What values and ideas do we live by?

Acceptance, Appreciation, Attention
Balance, Beauty, Boldness, Boundaries, Bounty
Caring, Communication, Courage, Creativity
Determination, Discipline, Discovery, Doing
Effort, Empathy, Enthusiasm, Exploration
Fairness, Family, Flexibility, Freedom, Friendship, Fun
Generosity, Gratitude, Growth, Guidance
Health, Honesty, Hope, Hugs, Humor
Imagination, Independence, Initiative, Integrity
Joy, Journey, Justice
Kindness, Kinship, Knowledge
Learning, Listening, Life, Love, Loyalty
Mastery, Mercy, Mindfulness, Miracles, Mystery
Nature, Newness, Noticing, Now
Openness, Optimism, Opportunity, Organization
Patience, Peace, Possibilities, Presence, Promise
Quality, Questioning, Quiet
Recovery, Resilience, Respect, Responsibility
Searching, Sensitivity, Serenity, Sharing, Spirit, Surprise
Tears, Thanks, Time, Transformation, Trust, Truth, Trying
Understanding, Unity, Us
Variety, Vitality, Vulnerability
We, Willingness, Wisdom, Wonder
You, Yes!
Zest

It Takes a Village

The African phrase, "It takes a village to raise a child," is now part of popular culture. This simple thought emphasizes that the whole community has responsibilities in providing an environment which nurtures the healthy development of each child.

This also means that parents aren't supposed to do this job alone. We all need a supportive network around us of family members, friends, and community services to help us raise healthy children.

Who are the people you look to for support?

Who are the people to whom you give support?

In the village, everyone feels a sense of belonging and connection. In the village, everyone's needs are met. No one goes hungry or wanting. In the village, the responsibility for raising a child and assisting in that child's development is shared by all adults.

We need to create a strong, caring community that supports all family life.

Life Skills December 3

Life skills are all those things we would like children to eventually be able to do on their own – good hygiene, cooking, cleaning up, laundry, managing their money, holding a job.

Life skills also include abilities that help us to have healthy, positive relationships – communication skills, listening, and conflict resolution.

Life skills help us to have fun and relax. Too much time spent working without fun and self-care is damaging to our overall well-being.

All of these skills help to create a successful life. We sometimes wish we could wake up in the morning and have mastered a new skill, but they are not learned overnight. All skills require lots of practice before they become healthy habits.

We can include children in meal planning and preparation. We can ask them to help us change the sheets on the beds. We can let children run the vacuum. We can encourage listening and communication when feelings are hurt. We can teach life skills and have some fun every day.

Holding Our Ground

"But Mom, everyone else does!"

Sometimes it feels like we are swimming upstream against a strong current. We have our own ideas about what is healthy for children. We have values that we want to maintain. And it seems like many other adults have given up.

Other children have no bedtime routines.
Other families don't eat together.
Their TV is *always* on.
Children are exposed to many things in the
    media.
They are left home alone for hours.

Each of these issues and many others can be frustrating for us. It is difficult to teach values to children amid these rapidly changing standards. But we can. We do this by the role model we provide and by the way we live.

"I know they do that at their house. We do
things differently here."

Children need love and limits. It is our responsibility to create a safe, caring environment.

Seen AND Heard

"Children should be seen and not heard." Where did THAT come from? Whose bright idea was this – to stifle the energy, enthusiasm, curiosity, and contributions of children? We all know someone who believed or still feels that children should be quiet in the presence of adults.

Children bring joy and delight to our lives. They bring smiles and giggles. They have concerns and questions. They have amazing ideas to offer!

Where are they going to learn about appropriate social interactions and how to behave around people, if not from us!?

Children learn to wait their turn, with an adult's respectful reminder. Children learn to interrupt politely, placing a hand gently on an adult's shoulder or arm. Adults can learn to ask for a child's opinion and include them in discussions. Sometimes children just want to watch, learning through observation.

Children learn how to behave politely and appropriately by being included in social gatherings.

Legacy of Love   DECEMBER 6

What are the most important, lasting gifts we can offer children? We are all unique, with our own values and strengths. Surprisingly, when you ask someone what special memories they have of their parents' love, it is often the small things that matter most. These special memories are tiny moments in time which cultivated the seeds of love –

Stories read at bedtime
Shampooing hair
Making cookies
Trips to the park
Doing chores *together*
Intimate conversations in the car
Laughter during family mealtimes
Hugs during hard times and whenever
A "thumbs up" at a school presentation

We are at our best when we are demonstrating our love and concern with the little things we say and do. At some time in the distant future, when children look back, what do you hope they will remember?

Trust Is Learned and Earned   DECEMBER 7

When a baby cries, we respond with the appropriate care. It may take several weeks for us to learn what the different cries mean, but eventually we figure this out. An infant learns to trust that we will respond. He is also learning to trust his own body and his ability to communicate his needs.

Trust is learned at other times as well. Children learn to

trust that we will pick them up from child care. They learn to trust that morning follows night and a good night's sleep. We learn to trust that they will finish all their homework. They learn to trust that we will follow through with a promised activity.

When a promise is broken or the truth turns out to be very different than expected, trust becomes shaky. To earn it back, consistency and dependability are necessary.

Loyalty DECEMBER 8

All siblings squabble over things: a parent's attention, toys, needing space from each other, "me first." But, an attitude of "kids will be kids" can sometimes give the idea to children that we think it's okay to fight and pick on each other. It's not. Children learn how to communicate and get along with others within the fertile soil of family life...or not.

We have the very important job of encouraging their loyalty to each other and the family. Loyalty is about strong emotional bonds, devotion to family, and looking out for each other. Our values can seem like very high expectations when children are fighting about the many insignificant things that seem so huge in the moment.

In the long term, loyalty is an important ingredient in the glue that binds us together as "family."

Compassion DECEMBER 9

To feel another's pain. To experience another being with love and understanding. To bring an open and tender heart to our relationships.

Compassion brings people together. We aren't meant to go our way alone. Human beings often choose to live with people for whom they care deeply. When life is difficult, we seek out people who care. Thankfully, many of us have the support of family and friends who accept us just as we are and encourage us to be all that we can be. Others of us look within to find that acceptance and unconditional love.

Children need our compassion as we respond to their mischievous behavior. They like knowing that we understand, having been children once ourselves. They make mistakes, and we make mistakes, too. Adult mentors help children learn to be empathetic and accepting of others. Compassion can shape our choices and guide our steps.

The Gimmies

For birthdays and holidays, children can become conditioned to receiving. Some children are accustomed to getting a physical reward at every turn. They soon come to expect it. With a room already full of "stuff" and a stack of presents in front of them, they rip through them all in a matter of minutes. They want, want, want...more, more, more.

Or children can learn to cherish what they have. They can be encouraged to move slowly when opening gifts and to acknowledge the giver with a "Thank you."

We can also live a lifestyle that reflects "less is more." Our example can help children learn to appreciate the things they have. We can raise children in an atmosphere of abundance, not an abundance of things, but of love. Children are often naturally generous. We can show them that when we give to others, we get back so much more in return.

Generosity

Young children demonstrate an innate generosity. If you let your toddler know that you're tired and need to rest for a few minutes, you will hear the sound of little feet as he brings you his favorite blanket and stuffed "lovey."

Then when the same child is ten or eleven, we may wonder where that sweet little one went. We ask for help with something and hear complaints and whines, "Oh, not again!" Remember, that generous toddler is still inside, somewhere.

When we notice the generosity, we can acknowledge it.

"The cat really appreciates you feeding her."

"Thank you for reading with your brother."
"That was thoughtful to give away those toys
you don't play with anymore."
"I am grateful you helped set the table."

We all like to know our efforts are appreciated. Our positive affirmation encourages generosity to grow.

Generosity is learned. We can model generosity by putting aside what we are doing and giving of ourselves to share a story or snuggle on the couch.

It Matters DECEMBER 12

So often we consider the big problems in the world today, and ask ourselves, "Does what I do or say really matter?" Global climate change; pollution and toxic environments; our shrinking natural resources of water, clean air, and energy sources; childhood obesity; violence in our streets; the impact of media on children; poverty's influence. So many challenges today seem impossible to resolve.

In spite of our frustrations, what we say and do still matters. There are things we can do to help. And children can be some of our biggest supporters.

School-aged children can be passionate about injustice. We certainly hear siblings saying, "Hey, it's not fair that he gets to do that and I don't!" These same children can also be tireless advocates for a neighborhood clean-up or efforts to recycle.

There are many small steps that can become bigger efforts. We can work with children to –

> Respond to each other with respect
> Recycle all cans, glass, and paper
> Pass on gently-worn clothes and toys
> Clean up the local stream
> Turn the TV off and play outside
> Write letters to officials
> Eat healthy meals together

When we are thinking about how to resolve a problem, children can surprise us with their creative ideas and their willingness to help.

Thank You December 13

Gratitude is good for the spirit. Gratitude is also good for relationships. When we focus on the positives and show our appreciation, it is really hard to get angry or stay angry. We can accomplish so much more when we remember what we are thankful for:

> The unconditional love of children
> Supportive friends
> A helping hand
> A bed to sleep in and food to eat
> A beautiful day
> All the things going *right* in our lives
> A "fresh start" to try again
> People and services that help us care for
>   children
> Opportunities for life-long learning

We can share our thankfulness with children openly and often!

> "Thanks for putting your dishes into the sink."
> "Your little sister likes it when you help her get
>   dressed."
> "I appreciate it when you remember to put
>   your dirty clothes in the hamper."

When we show our gratitude, it comes back to us in many ways. "Thank you, dad. You're the best!"

Me First! December 14

There's a race to get to the car first. They both want to sit in the honored front seat. Or first to get our attention. It is very normal for children to vie for our attention and scramble to be first in line when the "fun" is being dished out. They don't want to miss anything! And it's our job to help them negotiate this competition, especially if it starts to escalate into a fight.

Helping children manage their behavior is just one of the many demands that come up daily, pulling on our time, energy, and patience. When do you put yourself first? We shouldn't wait until we feel a "fight" coming on. If we feel our patience draining, it is time to slow down, put our feet up, and take care of "me first!" If we don't take care of ourselves, we find ourselves in the middle of a squabble with children because we are worn way too thin to respond calmly.

Just like we need to help children take turns being first, sometimes we need to say to ourselves, "Me first!" When we take care of ourselves, we are more likely to have the patience to work out things with children.

Anger Outburst! DECEMBER 15

You are focusing intensely on a task. You feel rushed to complete it by the end of an already exhausting day. Your child enters the room and asks a question. You snap, "What do you want?!" Angry reactions can flare up out of nowhere, and we overreact when we are feeling disappointed, overwhelmed, or tired.

Children are not out to get us. They do not deserve this kind of response from us. Our outburst is way over the top! Even if this is the fifth interruption after we asked to be left alone, we can still try to respond patiently.

If you are feeling overwhelmed and on edge, take a break. If you can't trust your response, take a time-out! Yes, we have things to do, deadlines to meet. But what is more important than our relationships? We can learn to manage our anger and respond with patience.

Reframing Our Setbacks

Nothing has ever been invented without first creating a few unsuccessful "flops." We haven't failed. No one's perfect. We need our mistakes. They give us opportunities to learn and grow.

A setback is not the end. It's a pause, a chance to gather our energies before we try again. Many experiences are difficult at first and become easier with time – writing your name, drawing a picture, riding a bicycle, completing a jigsaw puzzle, following directions.

Children get frustrated when things don't go as they had hoped. So do we. We have many opportunities to show them how to deal with these curves that life throws us. We can reframe our setbacks. Rather than letting our frustrations get the best of us, we can turn our setbacks into comebacks. Some things help us look at challenges as opportunities:

Patience – Learning takes time.

Persistence – We need determination to stick with it!

Practice – Many things start out difficult and become easier with time.

Progress – One step at a time, one day at a time, we can overcome a challenge and move forward.

Remember – A setback is just a setup for a comeback.

Waiting

Waiting is hard for all of us. It is especially difficult for children to be patient. They are growing and need to move, so it is hard for them to sit still and wait. Children become bored, because they need stimulation and activity. It's impossible for them to wait when they are anticipating something special and it just doesn't come quickly enough.

When we remember that waiting is hard for children, we

come prepared to help them out. We schedule our errands to plan for the least amount of waiting. If you know you are going to be out doing errands or waiting for a while, take along some things that will entertain and distract. Bring along snacks, books, and small toys and games. Play guessing games together, "I see something red. What is it?"

Waiting is difficult. Time drags when we are all miserable. Time seems to pass more quickly and we can all be more patient when we come prepared and make it fun.

Security Blanket DECEMBER 18

> She carries her ragged blanket with her
>   wherever she goes.
> He likes to sleep with one of your old
>   sweatshirts.
> Holding a four-inch piece of toweling helps
>   when she's tired.
> The once pink rabbit has been loved so much it
>   is now a dirty beige and has only one ear.

Many young children adopt an object as a "lovey." When they are frustrated, overwhelmed, or feeling insecure, this object helps to ground them. They can breathe easier and get through separations and transitions with this to anchor them to solid emotional ground.

We have security objects too, most notably our calendars or day books. Where would we be without our purse or wallet? We also find comfort in a favorite chair or cozy corner in our home.

Most children outgrow their dependence upon this object or trade it in for other things. We don't need to rush this or force the issue. We may need to set some limits about appropriate times and places.

We all need love and support during difficult times. This is not a sign of weakness. Finding a "security blanket" can be a healthy way of insuring emotional health.

We Have What We Need DECEMBER 19

Sometimes in the rush to accumulate all of the things we think we need to be comfortable, we forget that we have what we need right now.

Somebody loves us and we love them. Love really does help the world go round. Feeling loved and giving love help us feel enthusiasm for life.

Our family and friends are there for us. Some of us have very strong connections with our friends, while others have very close ties to family. Most of us have at least one special person whom we can look to for encouragement.

We live on an amazing planet. Even in the midst of all of the noise and congestion, flowers grow up through the sidewalk cracks. We can notice the dirty streets or the smiles on the faces of the people we pass.

Opportunities for learning present themselves all the time. Children learn from observing. They also need adults in their lives who demonstrate a positive attitude and show their appreciation.

We have resources that offer love, support, beauty, and opportunities for learning. We can complain about what we don't have. Or we can notice and appreciate things that bring us joy each day.

Surprise! DECEMBER 20

Life is full of surprises. We can be open to them and look forward to each wondrous new happening. Or we can hold tight to our way of doing things and close our eyes to discovery.

Most children choose surprise. They are full of surprises and appreciate wonder. Are you ready for amazement?

"Boo!" from around the corner

A new accomplishment

A lost tooth

A found treasure

Drawing a picture

An unexpected gift
Tying his shoes
Kindness to a pet
Making a bed
Standing up for a friend

Children do the unexpected. Then they learn to do what is expected. Balance really is possible. We can all learn to cherish a sudden splash of color in the sky or the smile of a stranger.

Make Believe   DECEMBER 21

One of the tasks of childhood is to learn to tell the difference between fantasy and reality. Once we reach adulthood we realize that there is sometimes a fine line between real and pretend. Our perceptions can be very different. Who's to say sometimes what is real?

Children have an endearing capacity for imagination. They believe in Santa and the tooth fairy. They believe there are monsters under the bed. They believe mom and dad are all powerful.

Here's where we can learn from them. We all need to make believe sometimes. We can imagine ourselves out of a boring situation. We can imagine a safer world. When we imagine and are open to possibilities, we can sometimes make things happen. Make believe can be fun. Make believe can help us feel safe.

Sometimes when we make believe, we come to believe in something.

You're Not Crazy   DECEMBER 22

You're feeling crazy. Nothing seems to be working out. You are feeling overwhelmed! Everything is difficult. A quiet, enjoyable day seems an impossibility.

You're feeling crazy, but you're not really crazy. Raising children is far from easy. We have bad days *and* good days.

We don't have to blindly accept the chaos. We can do things to put it behind us.

During these crazy times, *take a breath*. Get away, even if only for a few minutes.

Prepare to *start fresh*. Each moment we get another chance to try again, with patience and understanding.

We can examine our expectations. Sometimes we look at others' lives and they seem to be having more success. Though we often have hopes of perfection, this is an impossible dream. *Reasonable expectations* are much more reachable.

Sense of humor saves the day. Is this really so serious? Laugh out loud. Laugh together. Laugh!

Yes, life sometimes feels crazy. With a little effort, we can turn this into satisfaction and even joy.

Take Care of You   DECEMBER 23

You are valuable!

How often do we remember this? We get caught up in doing for others and responding to all of those things that keep calling out to us. How often do we really acknowledge that we are important? We deserve love and care.

When we don't take care of ourselves, we get stressed out. Then, we are more likely to respond to children with impatience. Yes, sometimes their behavior is out of control. But what are we teaching with our impulsive outburst? Our behavior is saying it's okay to yell, but it's not.

We can learn to deal with our frustrations differently. We can take a deep breath. Breathe in and feel your body slow down. Feel a different energy flow over you.

Kids depend upon us. They need us to understand them. They absolutely prefer positive energy coming their way. And to understand them, we need to take care of the little one inside us, too.

The kids in our lives are counting on us. Their healthy development is enriched by our calm presence.

The Spirit of Giving

Birthdays and holidays, most children expect to receive gifts. Sometimes they even make a list and hope to get *all* of their wishes filled. What do we get for them? What will satisfy their desires? What will please them?

More significant than any toy or game is our relationship with them. We give the gift of connection in many ways.

> *The Gift of Time* – Our presence is what really matters. Spending time together with no distractions, playing, talking, or just sitting.
>
> *The Gift of Patience* – So many people are in a hurry. What is that important? Children are. Their health and well-being are number one.
>
> *The Gift of Listening* – Oh, to be heard! To have someone who will pay attention to our words and feelings.
>
> *The Gift of Kindness* – We demonstrate kindness to others when we are cooperative, helpful, and generous.
>
> *The Gift of Caring* – Straight from the heart. We show care with hugs. We show we care when we meet their needs and consider their feelings.

The Best Gift of All

What is the best gift of all? What do children want most from us? Our time. Even though they may ask for things, what they really want is our undivided attention. They want us to play with them. They want us to listen to them. They want us to hold them.

If we put them off with "I'm too busy right now," they will go away and entertain themselves. But, is what we're doing right now really more important than spending a few minutes together?

Even a few minutes makes a difference. If we say, "Just a few minutes," and don't keep that promise, children learn that we can't be trusted.

But, when we give them our time, we are making some precious memories. When children look back on their lives, they will rarely remember a specific toy they got. But, they will often remember a favorite activity – reading together, playing cards, going on a hike, playing miniature golf.

We can find the time to make lasting memories. Time together is time well spent.

Magic Moments

As you are taking a walk in the park, you are able to leave the day's usual distractions long enough to focus on a toddler's careful exploration of the leaves in the path, the bugs under the rocks, the dog that runs up wiggling and sniffing.

While watching a TV show with your son about the caring commitment of elephants to the young ones in their family groups, you look at your son and notice he has tears of empathy in his eyes that match your own.

On a drive home from the dentist, when you aren't able to see her eyes, your teen talks about frustrations with school. You are able to listen and respond without judgment.

We never know when to expect these magical times. When we try to plan an opportunity to connect for an intimate sharing, it may not work.

Then, when we aren't expecting it, during a quiet moment, children open up. A window into the soul is revealed. But, only if we are willing to put our own busy lives on hold long enough to greet this child right here in front of us. And walk beside them for a few precious moments of deep sharing.

Another enduring gift we can give children is a better world. What kind of world are we leaving for them?

> We can create a world where people work together. We can do our best to resolve conflicts and strive for cooperation. Children learn from our kindness and flexibility.

> We can celebrate diversity and work toward a world where there is acceptance for all. Everyone has unique talents and abilities.

> We can be good stewards of the earth's resources. We can involve children in conserving what is here so they will have what they need to survive and thrive in the future.

> We can volunteer. There are many things that can be done to benefit others here and now. We are building a better world when just one child and one family is helped.

Children have an amazing capacity for generosity and kindness. They want to help others. Together we can build a better world today.

A Work in Progress

Wow! Is this the same child you were ready to "divorce" last week? Everything has been a struggle lately. You wondered if she would ever get it and learn that you had her best interests at heart. Today, you're grateful you got through that rocky period.

It is often true that right before there is a surge in new development and understanding for any of us, there is a period of discontent and confusion. Things just don't feel right. We're unsettled and uncomfortable.

Remembering this can help us be more supportive and patient during difficult times. We can trust that this will soon pass. Children often need time and space to work some things out on their own. We can slow down, relax our demands, and encourage consistent routines.

We are all a work in progress. These seemingly overnight changes teach us to have a little faith. With patience and support, challenging times pass and children grow!

Our Hands Hold the Future   DECEMBER 29

Look at the incredible, amazing curiosity in a child's eyes – so eager to drink the world in, touching, smelling, seeing, hearing, playing.

Each child is a ball of energy and possibility, holding hope for the future. And we hold the children. We can't know what the future will bring each child. But, our hands can hold them with reverence, awe, and appreciation. We can cherish the many gifts that each child will bring to the world. This is a mighty responsibility!

> Our healing hands can soothe a hurting child.
> Our capable hands can build a world where
>   children can learn and grow.
> Our creative hands can play with children.
> Our gentle hands can brush tangled hair and
>   calm tangled lives.
> Our careful hands know whether to help or
>   wait.
> Our protective hands can keep a child safe.
> Our strong hands can carry a child through
>   tough times.

Ours are the hands that hold a child. Our loving hands hold the future.

Hope for Tomorrow   DECEMBER 30

We have the hope for tomorrow right here in front of us. We need only open our eyes and hearts. We can touch eternity in a child's embrace. We can listen to music in a child's voice. Watch as she explores the world with wonder. It is difficult to change world events. But we *can* change our own heart. We can love each child into his potential. Tomorrow is right here in front of us.

> Let me gaze deeply into these clear eyes and acknowledge the questions in their depths.
>
> Let me enjoy the laughter that twinkles around the edges.
>
> Let me respond to yet another "Why?"
>
> Let me have the patience to hear and really listen.
>
> Let me wait for wisdom to emerge in this young one.
>
> Let me slow down and notice.
>
> Let me take the time to share this moment – seeing the extraordinary in the ordinary.
>
> Let me cherish the special moments of wonder, joy, curiosity, and pure pleasure with this child.
>
> Let me also be there for the times of hurt and frustration and pain.
>
> Let me learn from this child.
>
> Let me remember that I care for this child of tomorrow, today.

The Journey Continues DECEMBER 31

We have been on this year-long journey together. Guiding children can be challenging, stressful, and overwhelming. It can also be joyous and surprising. As we move into the new year, we can remember some of the ideas that can help us along the way:

> We are not *perfect* and we never will be. When we inevitably make mistakes, we can apologize and try again.
>
> We must *balance* the needs of our bodies, minds, and spirits as we also consider children's needs.
>
> *Openness, patience, and flexibility* help us face

the demands of the moment.

Listening is crucial to effective communication. Listen often.

We can *ask for help*. Children need the varied skills offered by a large network of supportive people.

We must *trust* that children can learn what they need to face their future. Our ongoing assistance and understanding help them negotiate the sometimes rocky path to adulthood.

Everyone deserves *respect*. As children continue to grow, even into adulthood, our *love* will always be needed.

Acknowledgments

I want to thank those who have helped make this book a reality.

My adult sons, Wade, Zak, and Gus, have been valuable teachers from the moments of their births. My husband Al has been a loyal partner who has always encouraged me to do the work I have felt called to do as a teacher and writer.

Before these 366 essays began to meet the page, Ellen Murray encouraged me to write a book. Once they were written, she offered tender feedback in the first edit.

In the early writing of these essays, my sister Susan was my biggest supporter, always offering suggestions and feedback to strengthen the message.

Conversations with my friend Isoke Femi led to the inclusion of photographs to visually tell a story. I am especially grateful for the expressive images and assistance from the talented eye of my friend Jane Kirn. Tera Antaree also offered several wonderful family photos. Bob Smith let me use a picture taken of him with Jennifer in La Primavera, El Salvador on a *Seeds of Learning* work party. Some of my own photos have also been included.

Over the years, I have read books, been to workshops, and talked with other parents. As a parent educator for the California Parenting Institute and an instructor at Santa Rosa Junior College, many have opened their hearts and lives to me. I appreciate the wisdom from all of these sources.

Thanks to Tera Antaree who helped with the most challenging phase for me, creating a graphic vision for the format of this book and preparing it for submission.

Finally, I want to thank my parents, Tricia and Gordon Martin, for giving me life and love.

Photo Credits

January	Tera Antaree
February	Glo Wellman
March	Jane Kirn
April	Jane Kirn
May	Tera Antaree
June	Jane Kirn
July	Robert Smith
August	Jane Kirn
September	Glo Wellman
October	Glo Wellman
November	Glo Wellman
December	Jane Kirn